COUNTRY AND SUBURBAN HOMES OF THE PRAIRIE SCHOOL PERIOD

With 424 Photographs and Floor Plans

by

Hermann Valentin von Holst

DOVER PUBLICATIONS, INC., NEW YORK

ACKNOWLEDGMENT

THE publishers of *Modern American Homes* wish to express their grateful appreciation of the hearty cooperation of the architects who kindly offered the products of their art and skill and furnished the plans and details which add so materially to the value of this work. They also acknowledge the assistance of those publications which are themselves doing so much to spread this desire for and appreciation of good home building throughout the country, and which have so willingly supplied the necessary material from their files.

The designs and studies which have been obtained directly from or by permission of the architects are indicated by the names which appear upon the plates. Other material has been secured through the cooperation of *The House Beautiful*, *American Homes and Gardens*, *Country Life in America*, *House and Garden*, *Western Architect*, *National Builder*, *Brick Builder*, and *Ladies' Home Journal*. The assistance of the latter publication has been particularly valuable, the designs published by its permission being shown on Plates 11, 12, 18, 22, 39, 43, 44, 52–61, 63–75, 77, and 78, Copyright 1909, 1910, 1911, and 1912, The Curtis Publishing Company.

A work of this kind must of necessity be only a compilation but it is hoped that the care and judgment which have been exercised in the selection of the material and the helpful comments of the author have resulted in a work of genuine merit—a real contribution to architectural literature as well as a stimulus to the seeker after a well-designed, well-built, and livable home.

Published in Canada by General Publishing Company, Ltd., 30 Lesmill Road, Don Mills, Toronto, Ontario.

Published in the United Kingdom by Constable and Company, Ltd., 10 Orange Street, London WC2H 7EG.

This Dover edition, first published in 1982, is an unabridged republication of the work originally published by the American Technical Society, Chicago, in 1913, under the title *Modern American Homes*.

The publisher is grateful to Mr. John J. Mojonnier, Jr. of the Oak Park Landmarks Commission in Oak Park, Illinois, for calling attention to this work and for making a copy of the original available for reproduction.

Manufactured in the United States of America
Dover Publications, Inc., 180 Varick Street, New York, N.Y. 10014

Library of Congress Cataloging in Publication Data

Von Holst, H. V. (Hermann Valentin), 1874-
Country and suburban homes of the Prairie School period.

Reprint. Originally published: Modern American homes. Chicago : American Technical Society, 1913, c1912.

1. Country homes—United States—Designs and plans. 2. Suburban homes—United States—Designs and plans. 3. Prairie School (Architecture)—Designs and plans. I. Title.
NA7561.V66 1982 728'.022'3 82-9514
ISBN 0-486-24373-7 (pbk.) AACR2

PREFACE

THE American home has undergone many changes in the last twenty years. The public is realizing more and more the value of outdoor life, as evidenced by the fact that large and small cities have country clubs, which are located in the most attractive spots of the region, forming in most cases the nucleus for a colony of country homes. The steadily improving means of transportation have also enabled the city man of moderate means to live at some distance from his place of business and enjoy all the advantages and comforts which are derived from a home in clean, fresh air, amongst trees, shrubs, and flowers.

It is interesting to note that this tendency towards country life—the "back to nature" movement—has produced, in a way, a new architecture which is very direct in its expression, and which is endeavoring all the time to eliminate the superfluous and fanciful. This new type of home has utility as its fundamental principle. It must embody all modern improvements and it must be economical in its general makeup. Another demand, which comes from the faculty of the average American to adapt himself quickly to his surroundings is that the modern country home shall seem a part of the scenery, a requirement which has encouraged the architect and the owner to use local materials in the buildings, wherever possible. Such modern improvements as the central heating plant and sanitary appliances have also helped considerably to change the general character of the American home, making the plan of the house a very flexible and interesting composition.

It is high time that this tendency to build an individual home be fostered and encouraged, as the over-crowding of our cities has resulted in an abundance of the poorer types of apartment and of tenement house, neither of which are conducive to a healthy development or to an increased efficiency of a nation. Such forms of dwelling are undoubtedly necessary, but there are so many instances where they are built by speculative interests without due regard to the demands of health and good sanitation that the people should be diverted, to as great a degree as possible, from the cities into surroundings where living conditions are more ideal. In our day especially, where concentration of energy has been developed to such a high degree, it is absolutely essential that the men and women, who are crowded together during the day time in very congested business districts, have the opportunity to enjoy a complete change of environment after the strenuous working hours.

It is with the idea of stimulating this increasing appreciation of good building and of comfortable country homes on the part of city people that this book has been published. By far the largest part of the publication shows houses of moderate cost, quite within reach of the great mass of modest salaried men. It has been the aim to illustrate these in as concise a form as possible, giving floor plans in most cases, in addition to exterior views of the building, and sometimes even interiors. Wherever possible, the cost of the building has been given, but attention should be called to the fact that the cost must be considered in connection with the date of erection of the building and the locality, inasmuch as these two factors will sometimes affect the cost considerably. The cost of building and labor has steadily increased of late years, and it is also a curious fact that building in or near a large city is considerably more expensive than building in a small town or in the country.

It has been the aim to show as large a variety of types and styles of homes as possible, not only as to plans, but also as to materials used. Special attention is called to "The Uniformity of Modern Floor Plans," Plate 45, and "Studies of Different Exterior Treatments of the Same Plan," Plate 46. An examination of these two pages will enable the reader to appreciate some of the fundamental points to consider when studying the plans of a house or when contemplating the building of a home.

It has been deemed advisable to include illustrations of a few larger homes in order to show that in the best type of these expensive residences the same feeling of simplicity is adhered to that constitutes the charm of the smaller house.

A few pages have been devoted to typical apartment houses of different sizes. It is only quite recently that the living porch has been made a feature of the flat, in an attempt to give it one of the most attractive features of the individual home. There is also a tendency in some localities to take away the box-like appearance of the ordinary flat building by giving it a pitched roof, and by increasing the size of the court on which the flats face. However, this fact is to be emphasized that not even the nicest flat can take the place of a home with a garden around it. The latter will mean somewhat more work, but is amply compensated for in the advantages that come from having a place where one can enjoy and appreciate the seasons of year in the open, and thus gain physically and mentally, to a remarkable degree.

H. V. VON HOLST

CONTENTS

The Two-Story Home

The One-Story Home

The Tent-House, Boathouse, and Garage

The Larger Home

The Apartment House

Miscellaneous Buildings

COUNTRY AND SUBURBAN HOMES OF THE PRAIRIE SCHOOL PERIOD

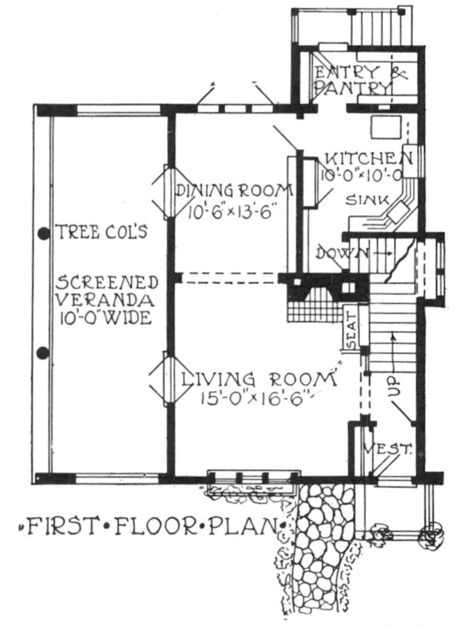

The Main Rooms Are Finished in Cypress Stained a Flemish Brown. The Walls Are Covered with Burlap

•SECOND•FLOOR•PLAN•

ROOF
BED ROOM 10'-6"×10'-6"
BED ROOM 10'-0"×10'-6"
CLOS.
CLOS.
BATH
DOWN
SEAT
CLOS
BED ROOM 11'-6"×21'-0"
LOUNGE

The Fireplace in the Main Bedroom Is a Very Desirable Feature

A Simple Home as Part of the Landscape

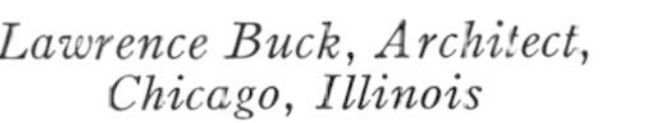

Lawrence Buck, Architect, Chicago, Illinois

THIS house was built by the architect for himself in 1904, at Rogers Park, Illinois. Since then he has built the new fireproof home shown on Plate 4. The plans and exterior are very simple and the arrangement, grouping of openings, and detail give it the artistic expression it enjoys. The exterior walls are covered with a cement stucco. The entrance feature is handled admirably, there being no attempt to make it a porch—just enough to give the necessary accent. The living porch, however, is made the feature of the house, provided with screens for summer time and movable sash for winter. The house was built for $3,000.

Closer View of Entrai

View of Fireplace and Cozy Corner of Living Room

An Attractive Small House in Harmony with Its Surroundings

Walter Burley Griffin, Architect,
Chicago, Illinois

THE usual square type of house is very monotonous, but in this design the square effect has been done away with by wide overhanging eaves, by a terrace forming a broad base, and by the grouping of the windows and a few well-disposed wood members. The roof shingles are left unstained, the walls are a grey plaster, and the woodwork is stained a red brown. Built for Mr. Frank N. Olmstead, Walden, Illinois. For plans and section, see plate following.

•WEST•ELEVATION•

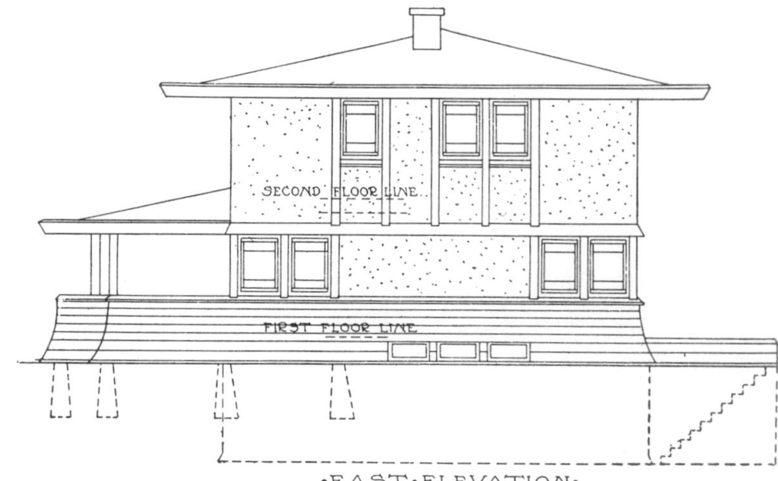

•EAST•ELEVATION•

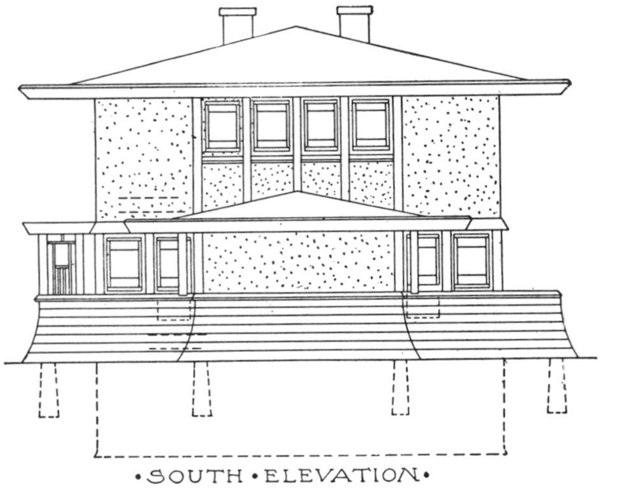

•SOUTH•ELEVATION•

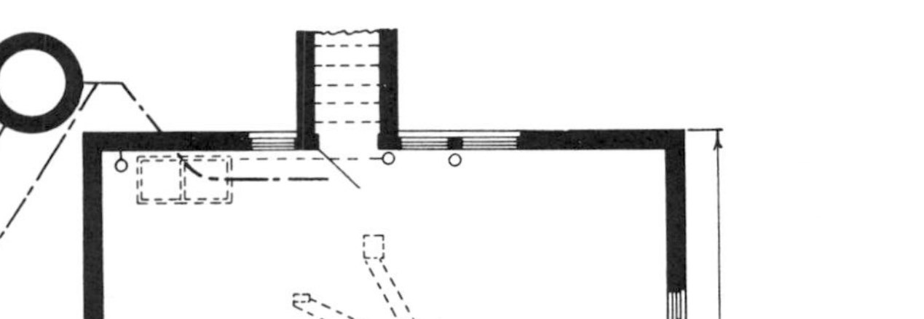

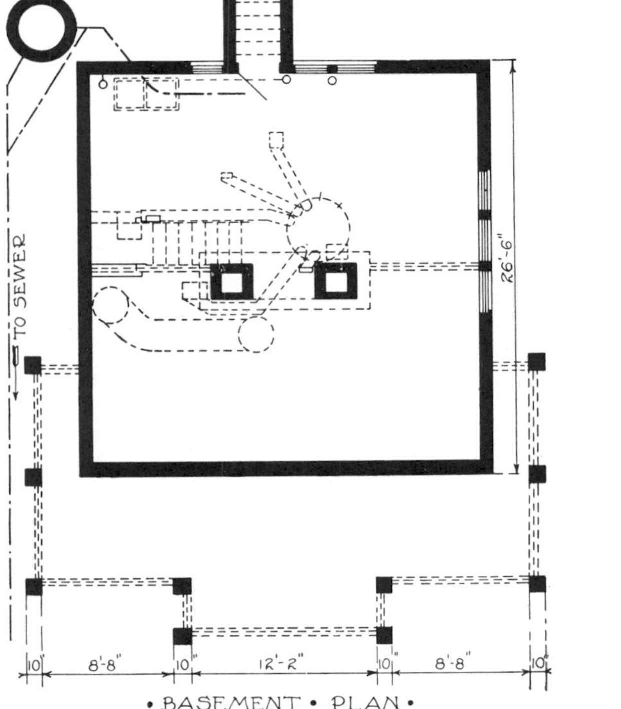

•BASEMENT • PLAN•

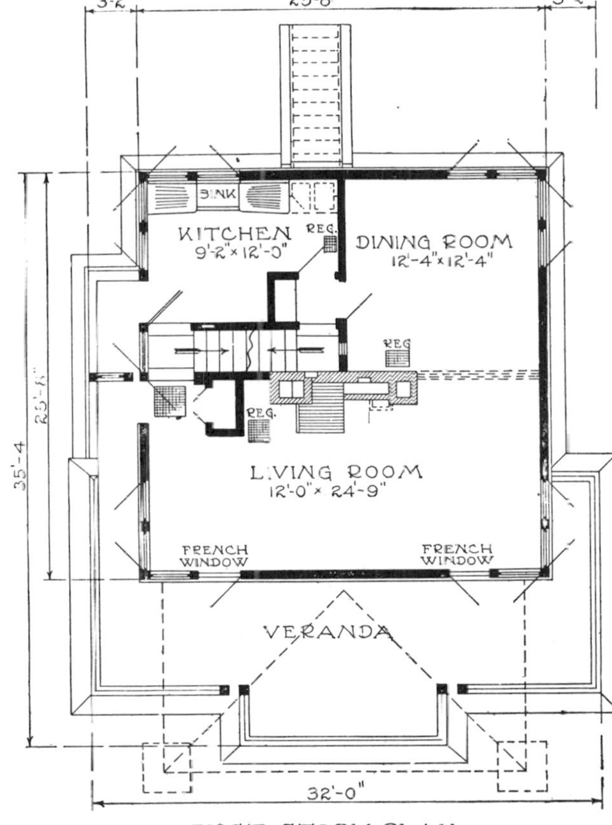

•FIRST•STORY•PLAN•

An Attractive Small House in Harmony with Its Surroundings

Walter Burley Griffin, Architect, Chicago, Illinois

THE living room and dining room are combined, the generous fireplace forming a kind of screen between. The windows are all casement, those in the first story being grouped at the corners while in the second story they are arranged in the center of the four walls. The inside trim is yellow pine and the second story floor joists are left exposed in the first story. The house was built in 1910 at a cost of $3,300. For exterior and further elevations, see plate preceding.

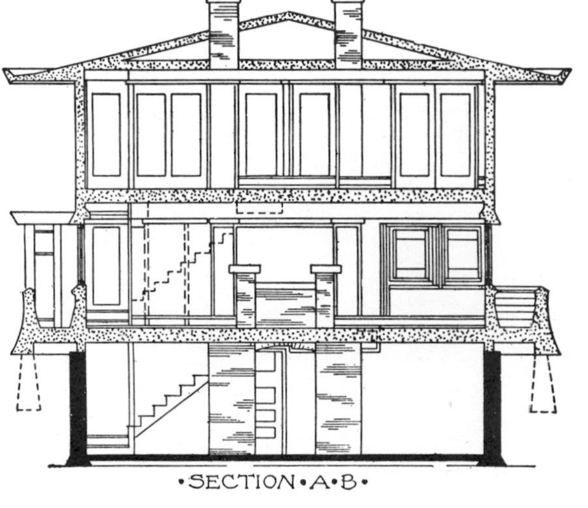

•SECTION•A•B•

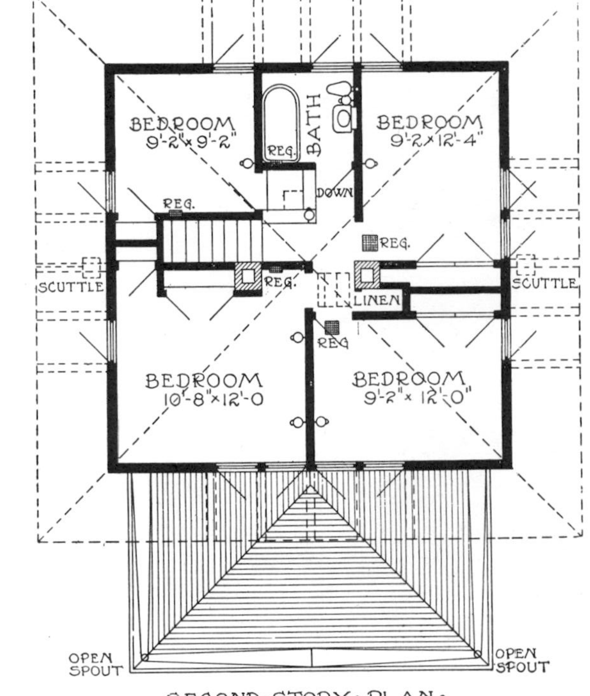

•SECOND•STORY•PLAN•

View of Mr. Buck's Residence Looking North, Showing the Screened Porch

The Walls of This Fireproof House Are of Hollow Terra Cotta Blocks, Plastered Outside and Inside Direct on the Tile. The Roof Covering Is a Flat Combination Shingle Tile

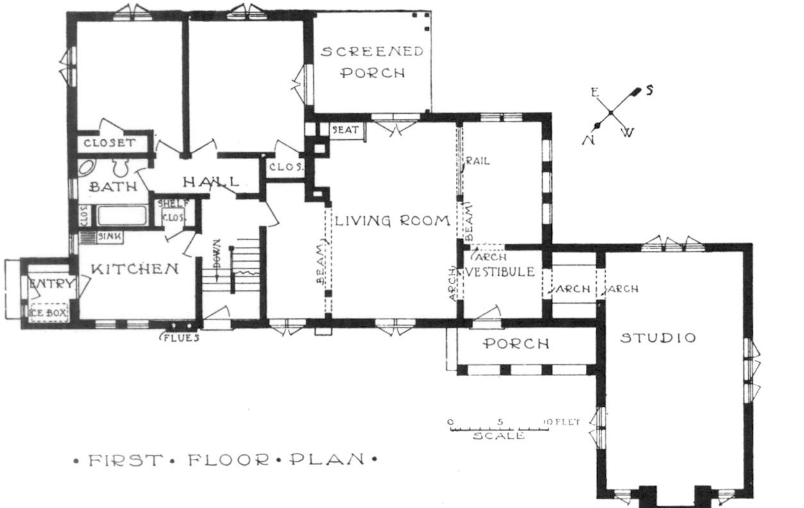

An Interesting Fireproof Dwelling

Lawrence Buck, Architect,
Chicago, Illinois

THIS house, which is the home of the architect at Ravinia, Illinois, is a most interesting example of absolutely fireproof construction. On the inside the wood trim has been reduced to a minimum by having plaster jambs, the door openings being in some cases capped by unique brick arches. The floors of the kitchen and bedrooms are of maple, and all of the remaining floors of concrete with cement base. It was built in 1911 at a cost of about $6,500.

Interior View Showing the Possibilities of Artistic Development with Fire-Resisting Materials

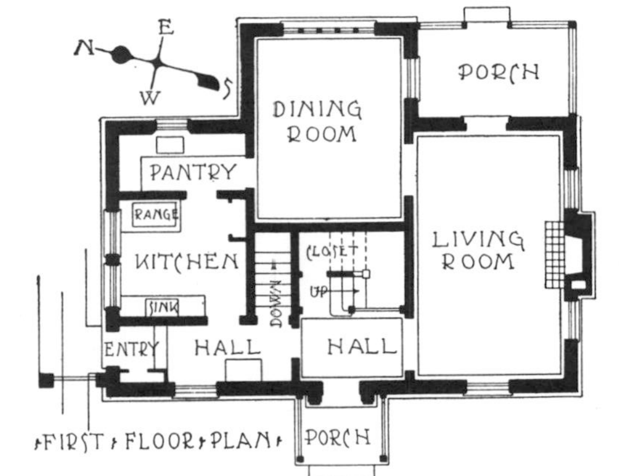

A Fine View of the Garden Is Had from the Dining Room

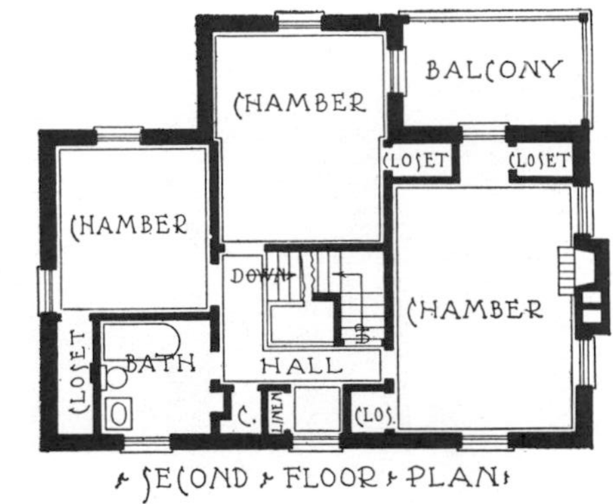

The Central Stairway Makes a Small Hall Upstairs Possible. The Maid's Room and an Ample Storeroom Are on the Third Floor

Compare the Window and Porch Treatment with That of the Brick House Shown on Plate 6

An Excellent Type of Stucco Country Home with Decided Colonial Feeling

Oscar C. Gottesleben, Architect, Detroit, Michigan

THE brick house shown on Plate 6 is of the same plan and dimensions, the difference in the two houses being in the exterior treatment and in some of the interior finish. The conjunction of the agreeable and the practical has been a condition that was constantly kept in mind while building this little place on a corner city lot 50 feet × 171 feet in size. Its itemized cost is as follows: Masonry, $1,900; carpentry, $1,450; painting and glazing, $175; plastering, $228; tiling, $44; galvanized iron work, $54; electric wiring, $55; electric fixtures, $80; hot-water heating, $400; hardware, $75; decorating, $125; walks, fence, and sodding, $140; plumbing, $365; total, $5,091..

Note the Difference in This Adaptation of a Salem Doorway and Lattice Treatment with That on Plate 6

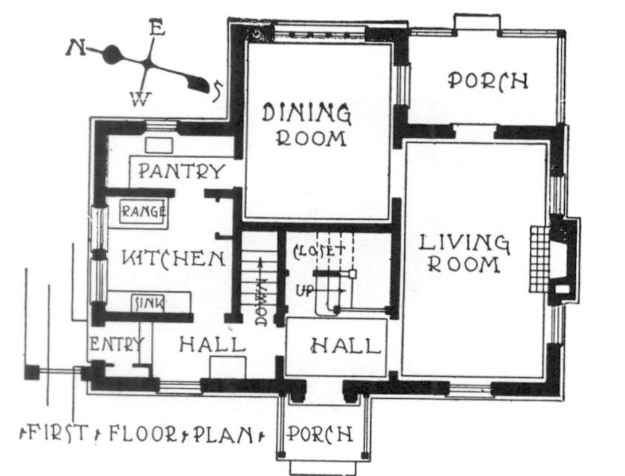

Very Little Room Is Wasted on the Hall Space. The Main Hall Is But 5 Feet by 8½ Feet

A View of Two Houses Built from the Same Floor Plans. The House in the Background Is the One Discussed on Plate 5

Having the Stairway in the Center Gives Room for Three Large Chambers Upstairs

A Brick House of Simple But Dignified Design

Oscar C. Gottesleben, Architect, Detroit, Michigan

THIS is an example of a substantial house of the colonial type.

The plan and dimensions are the same as those of the stucco house shown on Plate 5, the only difference being in the exterior, with minor changes in interior finish. The two houses make an interesting study of the effect of different materials and different roof contour. The exterior of the brick house has a gable roof while that of the stucco house has a hip-roof and a dormer in front. In the matter of plumbing, the fixtures are all about one "stack," or main drain and ventpipe, so that economy is carried to a point of perfection in that respect. The house is the residence of the architect. Its cost is similar to that given on plate preceding.

The Rear of the House Presents as Dignified an Appearance as the Front

Climbing Roses Will Cover the Arbor at the Front Door

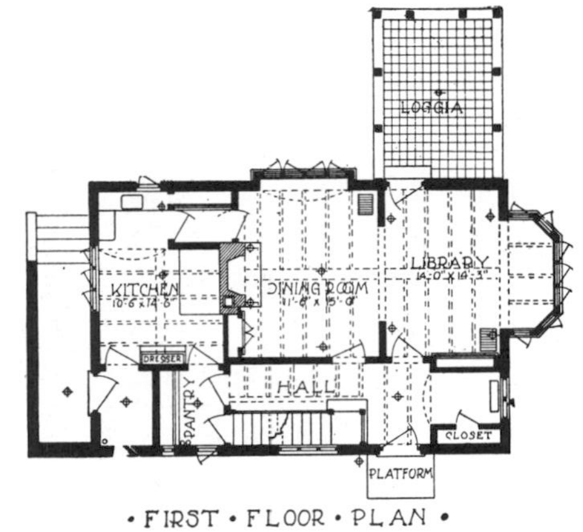

• FIRST • FLOOR • PLAN •

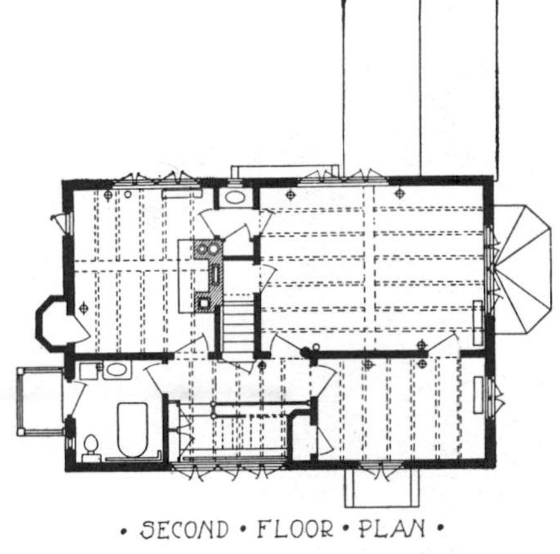
• SECOND • FLOOR • PLAN •

A Wayside Modern Home with All the Charm of an Old English Cottage

Joy Wheeler Dow, Architect, Summit, New Jersey

THIS house, which was built for Mrs. Elizabeth G. Dow, shows what can be accomplished by a clever adaptation of the design to the natural contour of the land, and by a careful study of the requirements of the different rooms in the house. The walls are of hollow tile plastered which, with the thick slate used on the roof, makes the outside of the house practically fire-proof. The loggia has a floor of red quarry tile. Built in 1910 at a cost of about $8,500. For interiors, see plate following.

The Porch Treatment, the Dining Room Bay Window, and the Lattice Work All Serve to Reduce What Would Otherwise Be a Stilted Appearance of the Back of the House

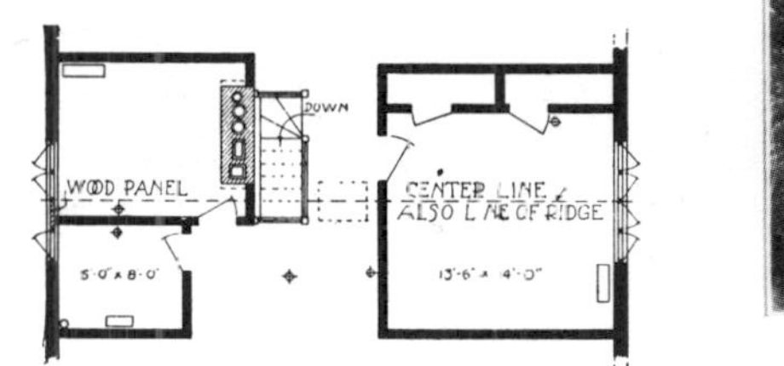

• THIRD • FLOOR • PLAN •

The Use of the Plain Wall Enclosing the Kitchen Yard Adds Great Charm to the Composition

Bay Window and Bookcase in Living Room. The Wood Wainscoting and the Exposed Ceiling Beams Give the Rooms an Air of Solid Comfort

A Quaint Chimney Piece

Bedroom Interior. The Inside Shutters Are Very Serviceable and Do Not Get Out of Order as Quickly as the Modern Shade

Fireplace and Bay Window in Dining Room

A Wayside Modern Home with All the Charm of an Old English Cottage

Joy Wheeler Dow, Architect, Summit, New Jersey

THE homelike quality in this house is very evident. The architect has a keen appreciation of the effective simplicity of the English country house and has adapted it to the modern requirements. The leaded glass windows are very effective and the same design has been repeated in the doors of the bookcases. For plans and exterior views, see plate preceding.

Clothes Yard and Kitchen Entry

View from Lake Oconomowoc. The House Faces South, Overlooking the Water

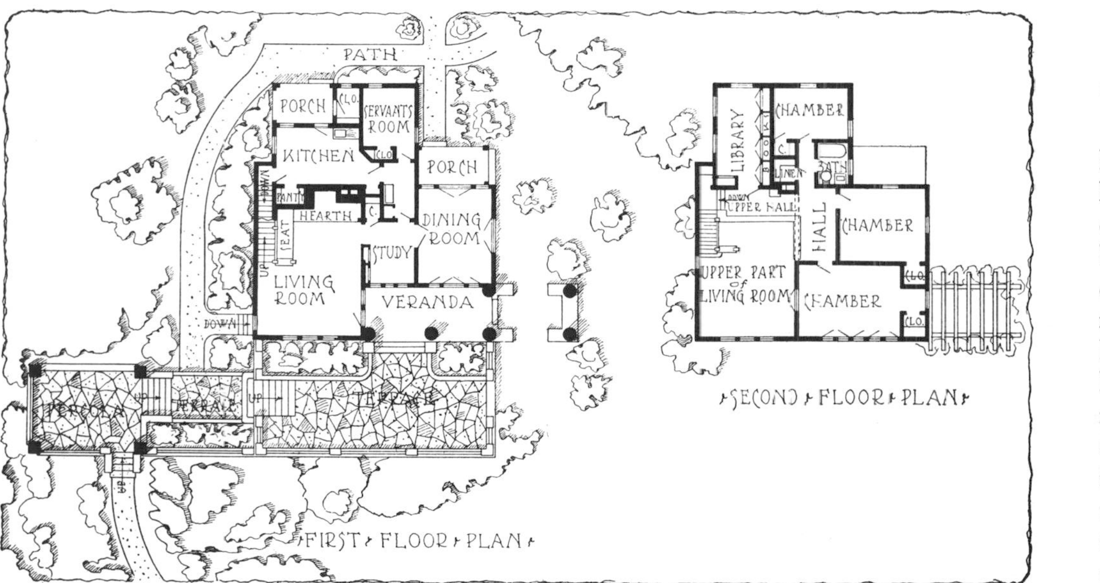

From the HOUSE BEAUTIFUL MAGAZINE

An Architect's Home

Alfred C. Clas, Architect,
Milwaukee, Wisconsin

THIS is a fine example of the possibilities of simple country house architecture, and shows excellent handling of a plaster house. The value of garden features to the design has been recognized by the owner and developed. The varied window treatment gives a picturesque quality to the house. This charming home, which is located on the north shore of Oconomowoc Lake, Wisconsin, about 35 feet above the level of the water, was built in 1907. The cost, including the terrace, electric lighting plant, lighting fixtures, and complete system of plumbing and heating, was $8,000.

The View of the Two-Story Living Room Shows the Attractive Fireplace and Balcony Above

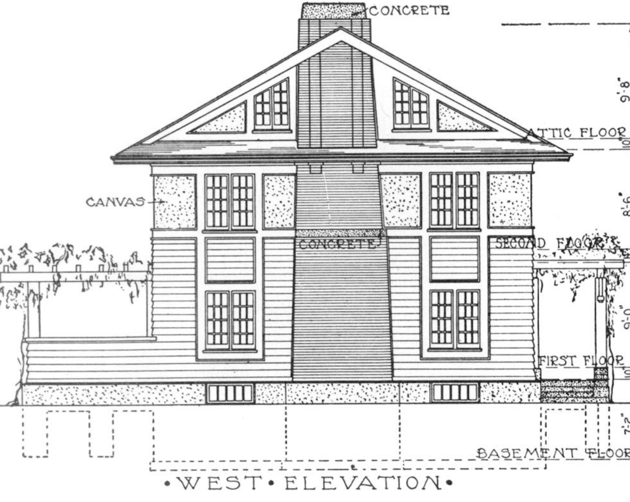

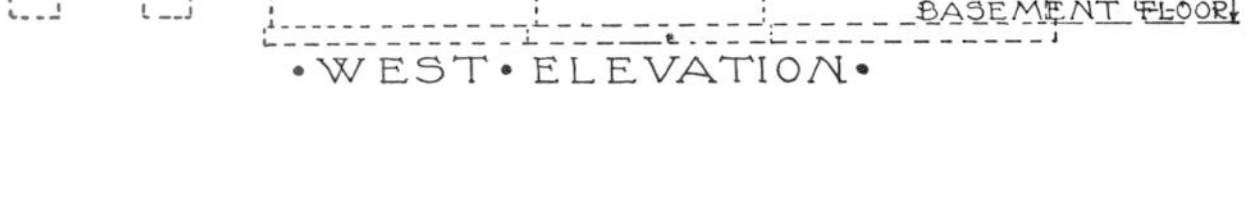

•WEST• ELEVATION•

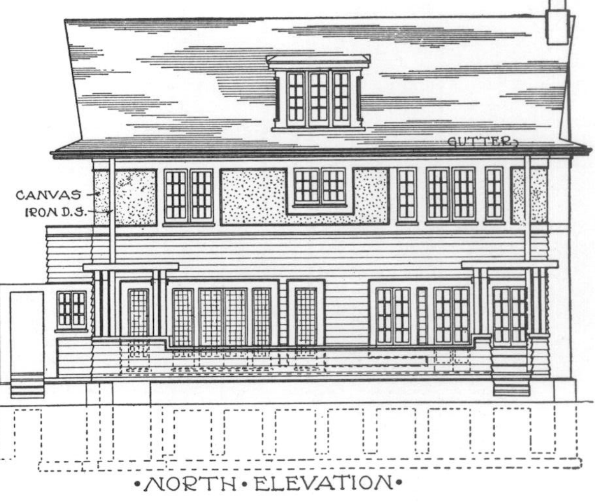

•NORTH• ELEVATION•

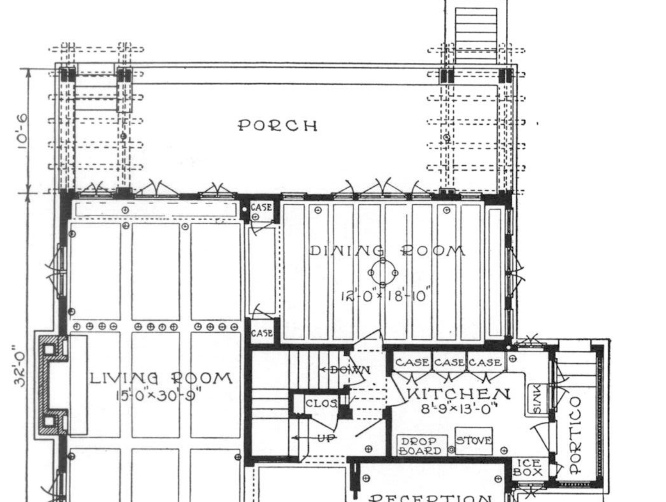

•FIRST• FLOOR • PLAN•

A Beautiful Type of Modern Suburban Home

Tallmadge & Watson, Architects, Chicago, Illinois

THIS residence of Mr. Elias V. Day, River Forest, Illinois, is an excellent type of modern home architecture. It shows an interesting treatment of the exterior finish with wood boarding, vertical boards running into the second story and tying the compositions together. The light panels in the second story are covered with canvas having a pebbled finish resembling plaster. This is cheaper than plaster and practically as effective. The house was built in 1907 and cost about $6,300.

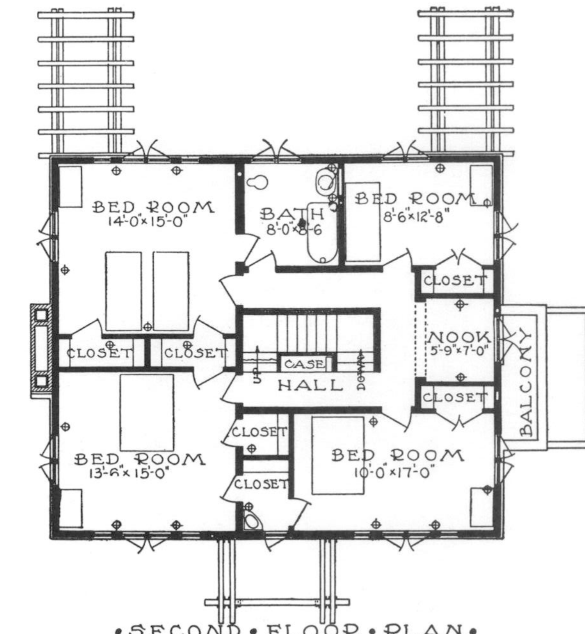

•SECOND • FLOOR • PLAN•

Rear View Showing Terrace and Porch on Which Living Room and Dining Room Open

A Quaint Old-Fashioned House

Designed by Charles Barton Keen and Frank E. Mead

THIS house, the residence of Mrs. Robert Holmes, Moorestown, New Jersey, impresses one with its old-fashioned atmosphere in every detail. The plainness of the front is broken by the little gable over the entrance and the narrow porch roof. The rear of the house shows by far the better effect, with the porch, the quaint little hedge, and hit-and-miss stone steps down the terrace. In order to utilize the porch to best advantage, the living room and dining room lead directly to it through French windows, thus throwing the kitchen area to the front of the house. The dormer window and the other window openings in the long sloping roof at the rear afford excellent light to the two principal bedrooms. For interiors and floor plans, see plate following.

The Old-Fashioned Entrance Is Most Inviting

View of Front of House and Big Chimney

Interior of Dining Room. The Simple Woodwork and Wall Paper Harmonize Well with the Furnishings of the Room

A Very Attractive Living Room. The Unfinished Flooring and Timbers of the Second Floor Make an Effective Beam Ceiling

A Quaint Old-Fashioned House

Designed by
Charles Barton Keen and
Frank E. Mead

IN the comfortable living room there are many unusual and individual touches. The floor is of brick laid on a sand base, thus making a floor which is warm in winter and cool in summer. The fireplace is of exceptional breadth and with the cozy high-back chimney seats gives a quaint and pleasing charm to the room. The design of the dining room is very well carried out. For exterior views see plate preceding.

PORCH
DINING-ROOM 10'0" X 14'6"
PANTRY
LIVING-ROOM 19'4" X 24'4"
SEAT
SEAT
KITCHEN 10'4" X 13'10"
UP
HALL
DOWN
SEAT
SEAT

First Floor Plan

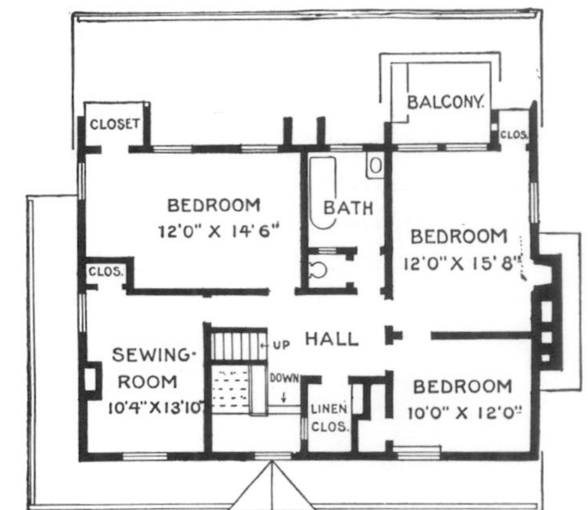

Second Floor Plan

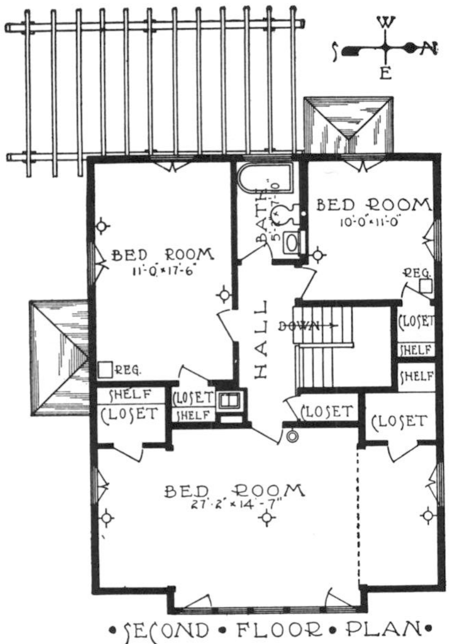
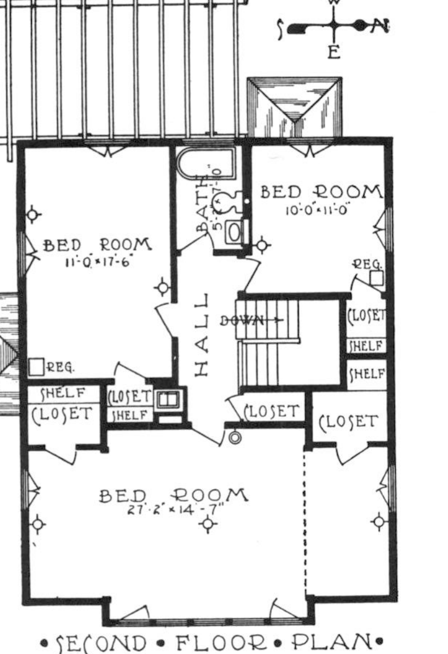

West End View Showing Pergola Porch

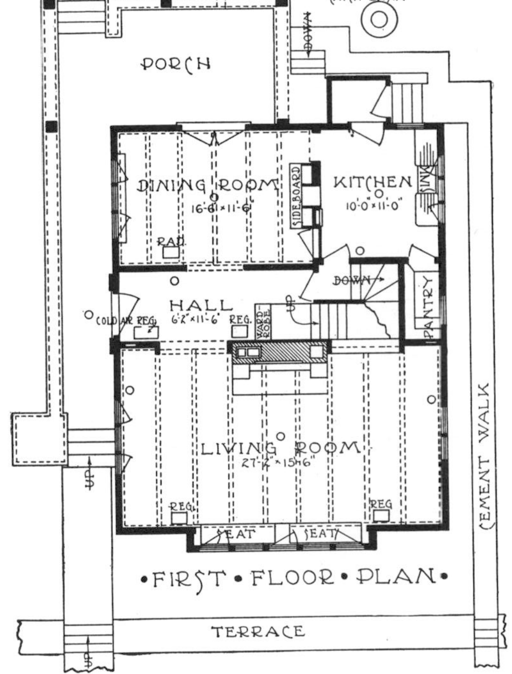

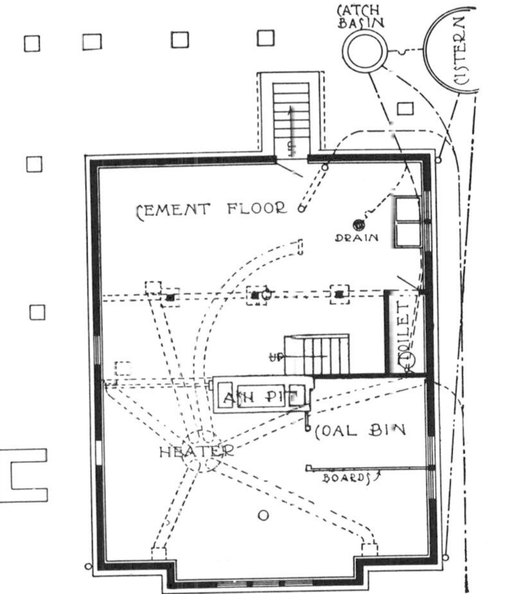
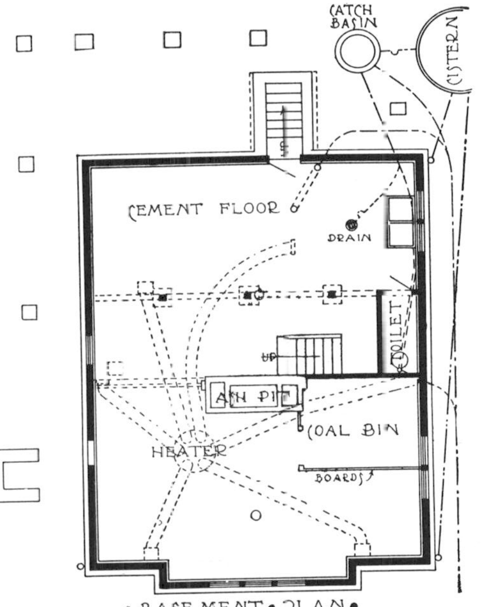

A Modern Suburban Home with Original Treatment of Exterior

Henry K. Holsman, Architect,
Chicago, Illinois

THE base course is of rough cast plaster; the walls above this are of board and batten alternating with a floated stucco finish in the second story. The living rooms have yellow pine finish and floors; the bedrooms, white wood finish with yellow pine floors and birch panel doors. The house was built in 1907 for Mr. Arthur V. Fraser, Elmhurst, Illinois, at a cost of $4,300.

A Low-Cost Suburban Home

Von Holst & Fyfe, Architects,
Chicago, Illinois

THIS house has been worked out very carefully to make it as compact and comfortable as possible. The exterior has wide boards and narrow boards alternating up to the second story windows, stained a rich brown, while the frieze above is of stucco. The building faces northeast. The rear living porch is provided with screens and sash, and is accessible from the play room and the living room. The sleeping porch is used throughout the year. The living room and dining room are combined, while the inglenook makes a delightful feature. The living rooms are trimmed in fumed oak, the bedrooms in birch, the bathroom in white enamel, and the kitchen in birch. The floors in the living room are of red oak, in the bedrooms of beech, and in the kitchen of composition. The house was built at Tracy, Illinois, in 1912, for Mr. Maurice LeBosquet at a cost of $7,700 including sidewalks, but not the architects' commission.

Rear of House with Glazed and Screened Living Porch Below and Sleeping Porch Above

Front and Side View of House Showing Entrance Porch

• FIRST • FLOOR • PLAN •

Living Room Looking Toward Dining Room End and Showing Inglenook at the Right

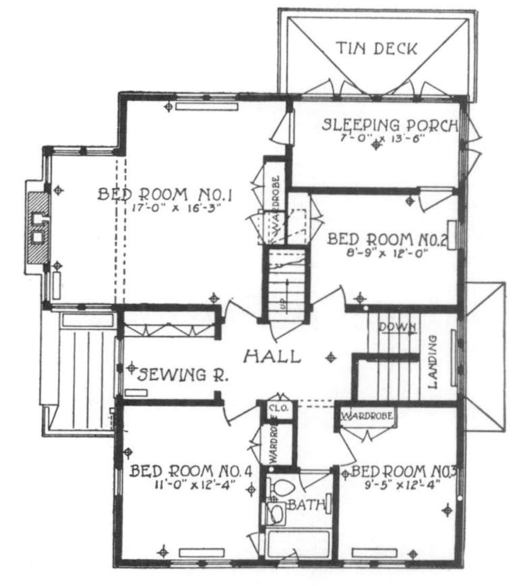

• SECOND • FLOOR • PLAN •

Frame and Plaster Residence of Remarkably Low Cost

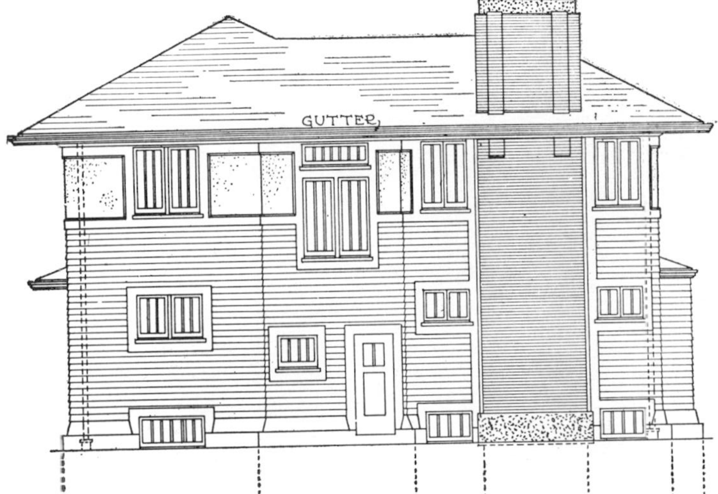

•FIRST•FLOOR•PLAN•

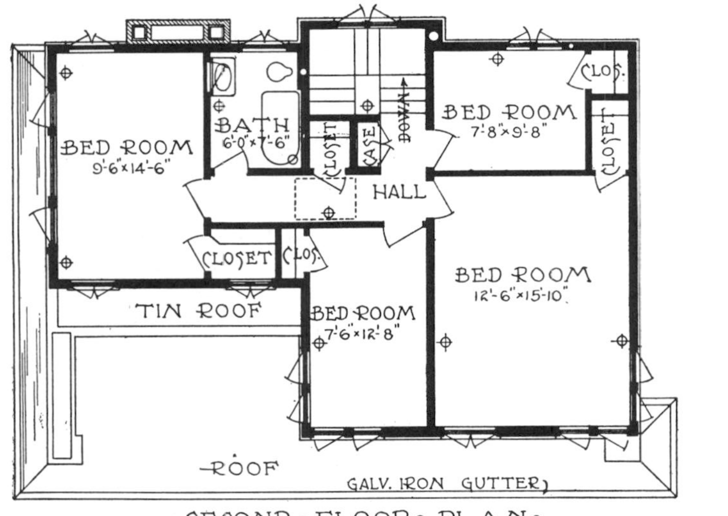

•SECOND•FLOOR•PLAN•

A Modest Suburban Residence with Excellent Lines

Tallmadge & Watson, Architects, Chicago, Illinois

THIS residence, which is the home of Mr. Gustavus Babson, Oak Park, Illinois, is a successful attempt on the part of the architects to solve the problem of the high cost of building. Its architecture was determined entirely by considerations of economy both in the materials used and in the method of putting them together, regardless of precedent. The rough character of the material harmonizes with the strong design. Narrow boarding is used on the lower part, while the panels in the second story are of pebbled roofing felt which resembles plaster. The interior trim is plain birch. The house was built in 1906 at a cost of $4,600.

GUTTER

•NORTH • ELEVATION•

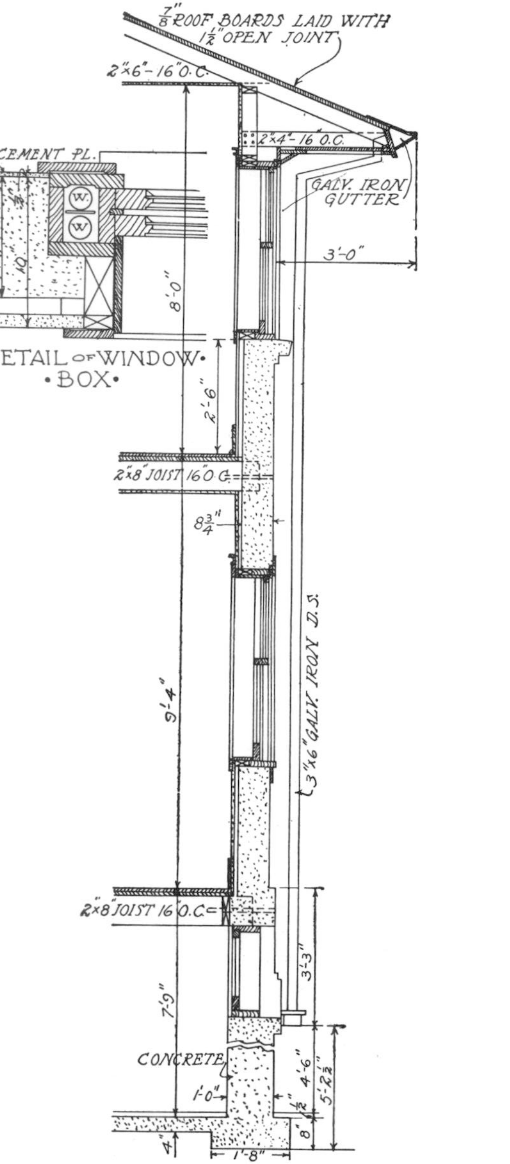

A Solid Concrete Country House

Vernon S. Watson, Architect, Chicago, Illinois

QUIET lines and a few touches of interesting detail, such as the porch rail and the wood screen, produce a pretty effect about this country house, the residence of Mr. Wyatt-Cronk, Oak Park, Illinois. The screen is built to hide the working space in the back yard. The wide overhang of the shingled roofs and the setting of foliage give a restful look to the house. Plaster makes the best possible background for trees and shrubs. For elevations and floor plans, see plate following.

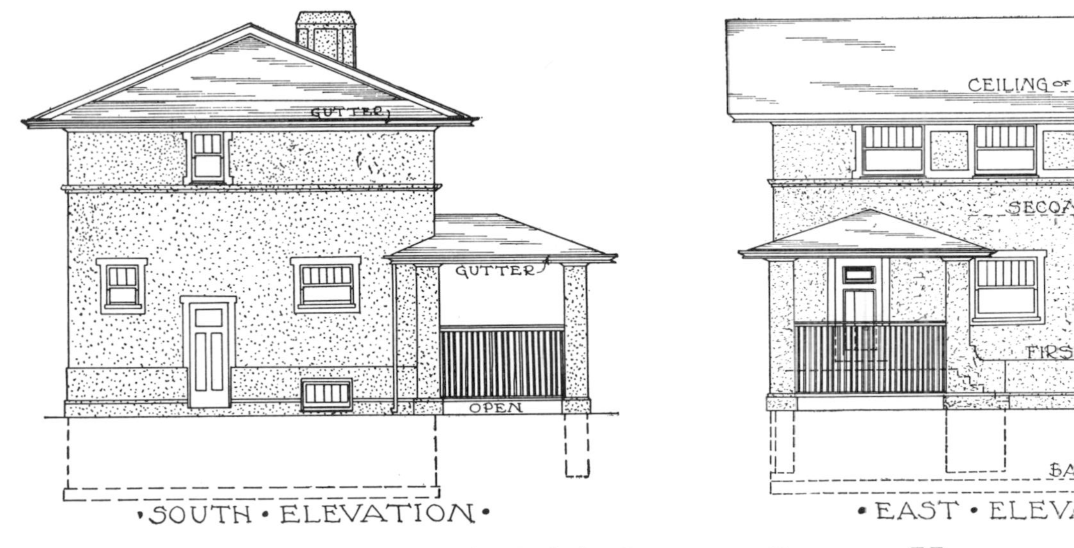

•SOUTH • ELEVATION•

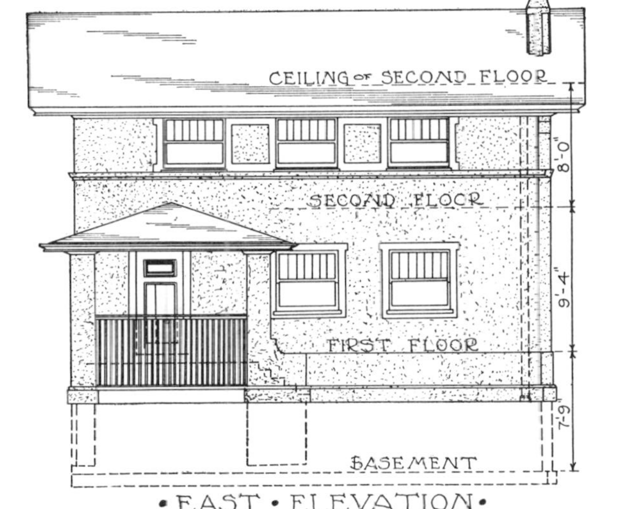

• EAST • ELEVATION•

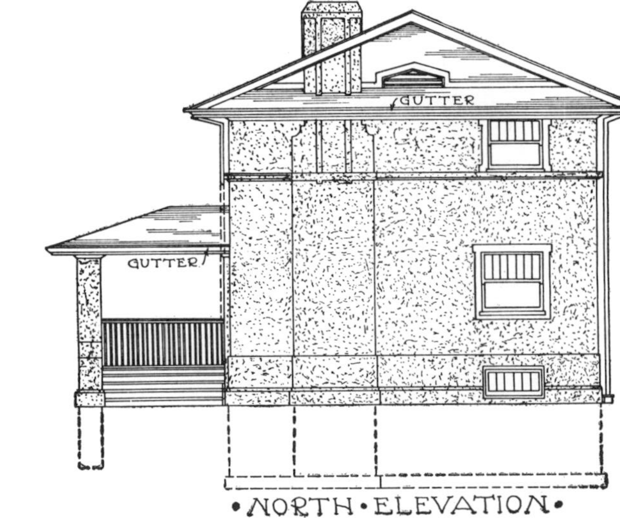

•NORTH•ELEVATION•

A Solid Concrete Country House, *Vernon S. Watson Architect, Chicago, Illinois*

THIS is a solid concrete house with a cement plaster on the outside and the interior trim of pine. The plan of the first floor especially is very economical giving the living rooms the maximum available space. The house was built in 1906 at a cost of $3,000. For exterior view and detail section, see plate preceding.

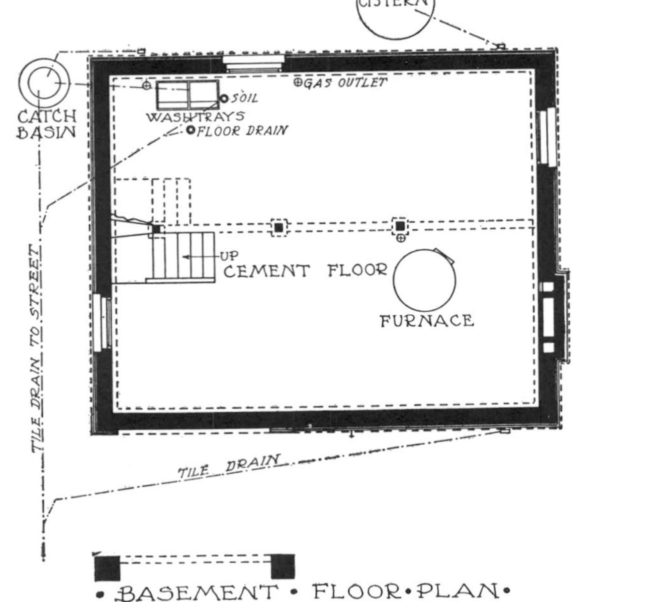

• BASEMENT • FLOOR•PLAN•

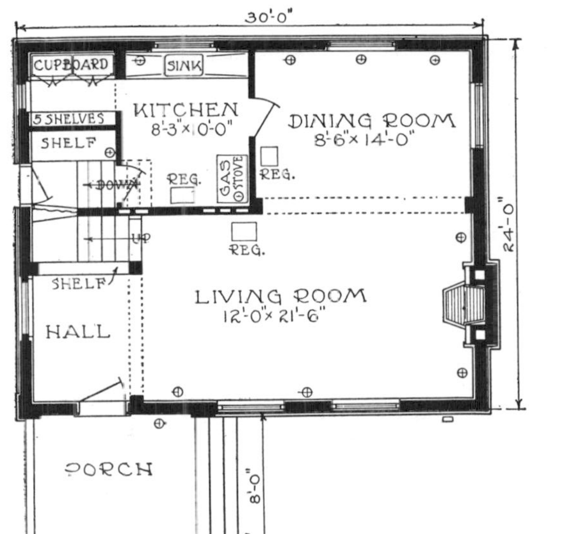

•FIRST • FLOOR•PLAN•

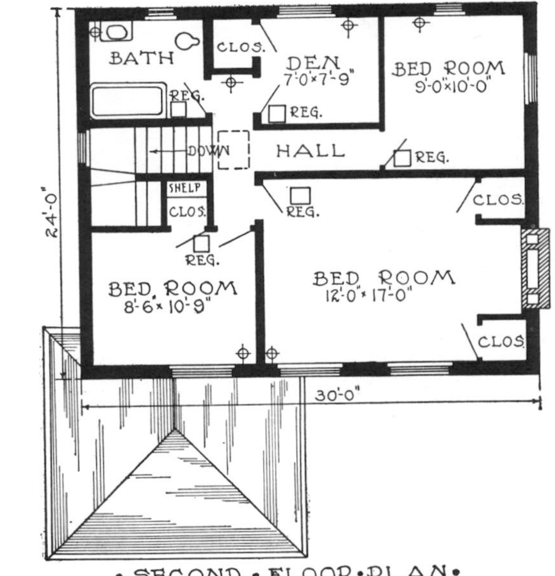

• SECOND • FLOOR•PLAN•

A Country House with an Old-Fashioned Effect Which Is Very Charming

A Small, But Well-Arranged Home At Moderate Cost

Designed by Adden and Parker

THE united efforts of architect and owner have produced a house of marked individuality at small cost. The exterior is shingled and painted white with green shutters which, combined with the little entrance porch and the fine broad living porch, give it the quaint charm it enjoys. This is further enhanced by the climbing roses, the window boxes, and other well-placed foliage about the dwelling. The interior arrangement is excellent, the big sweep through living room, hall, dining room, and porch being very effective. While the gambrel roof gives the low effect characteristic of this type of house, the use of the dormer windows makes the second story as roomy as the first. The house cost $3,027.

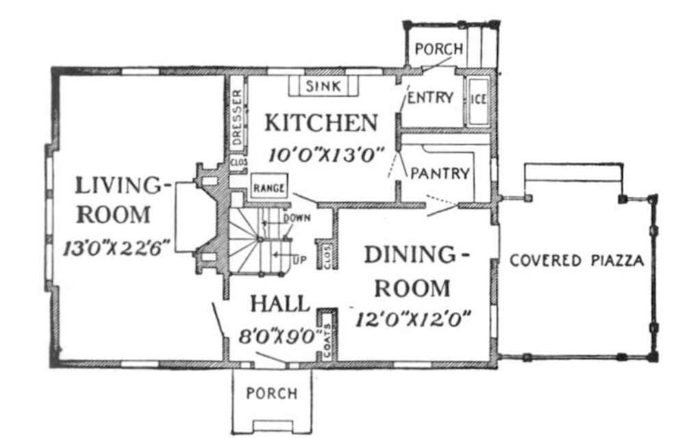

First Floor Plan

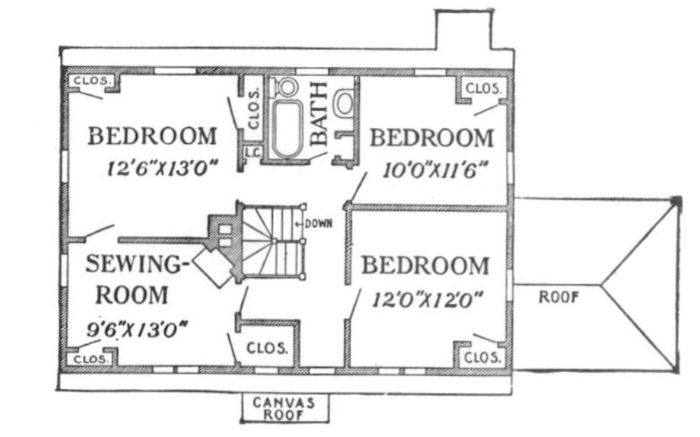

Second Floor Plan

PORCH
PANTRY
ENTRY
ICE BOX
DOWN
CHINA
KITCHEN
10'-6" × 10'-6"
SINK
RANGE
DINING ROOM
12'-0" × 14'-0"
PASSAGE
LIVING ROOM
15'-0" × 23'-0"
VERANDA
FLOWERS
N
E
W
S

• FIRST • STORY • PLAN •

An Inexpensive Frame House of Good Design

Charles E. White, Jr., Architect, Chicago, Illinois

THIS house, the home of Mr. Robert Kermen, Oak Park, Illinois, is an example of a very simple and compact design as may be noted from a study of the floor plans. The arrangement of the windows is particularly good in that it affords good cross ventilation in each room. The open character of the lower floor is also exceptionally attractive. The exterior walls are covered with siding; the roofs, with shingles. The house was built in 1907, at a cost of approximately $3,000.

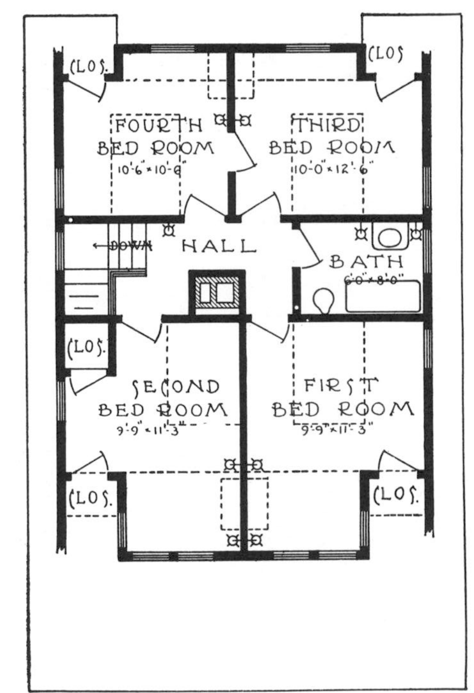

• SECOND • STORY • PLAN •

Plan of First Floor and Grounds

A Pleasing Design with Unique Window and Roof Treatment. The Enclosed Veranda Is Exceptionally Fine

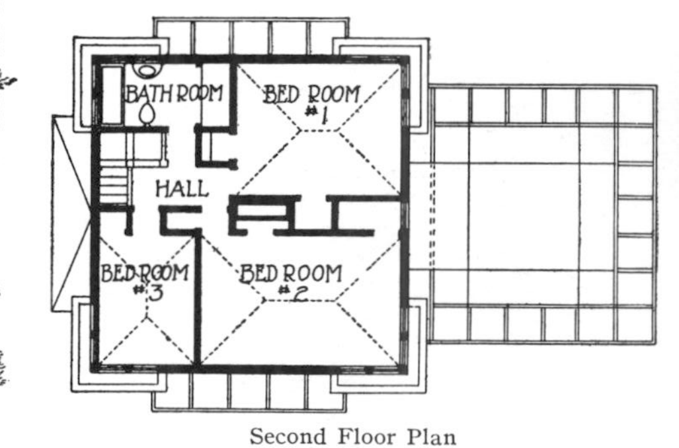

Second Floor Plan

Living Room with View of Veranda

A Tile and Plaster House of the Square Type

Walter Burley Griffin, Architect, Chicago, Illinois

THIS house, the residence of Mr. Harry E. Gunn, Tracy, Illinois, was built in 1911. The exterior walls are of hollow terra cotta blocks plastered outside and inside directly on the tile. The outside plaster is grey; the wood trim, a ruddy brown; and the sash, an orange color. The roofs are covered with canvas decks. The interior is finished in white oak, the beams shown on the plan being exposed structural beams. Cost $6,000.

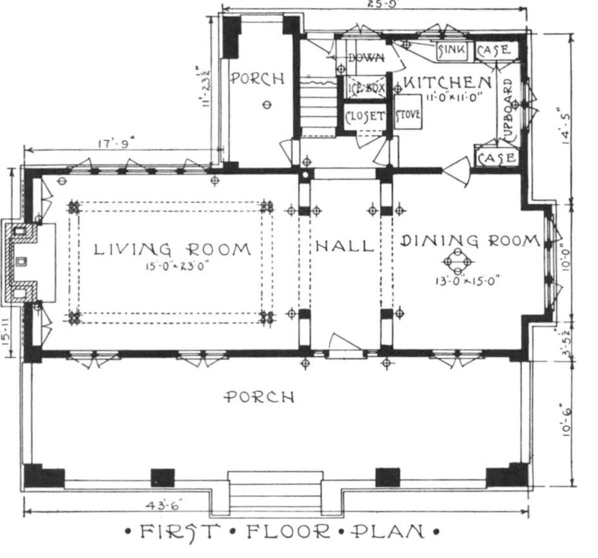

The Big Broad Porch, the Terraced Lawn, and the General Air of Comfort Make This Home Look Most Inviting

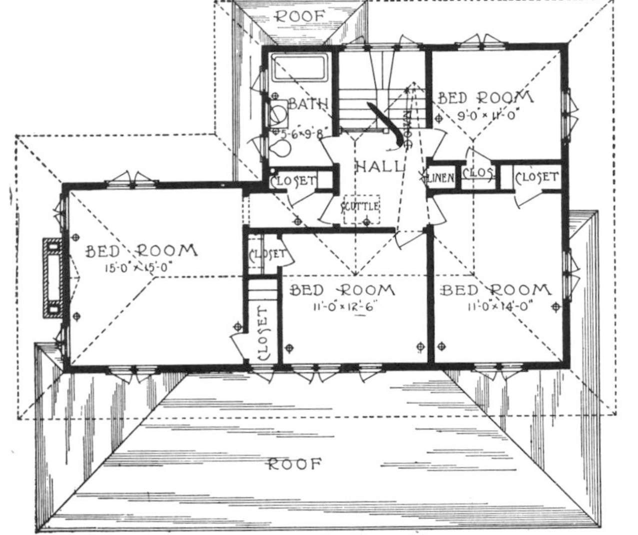

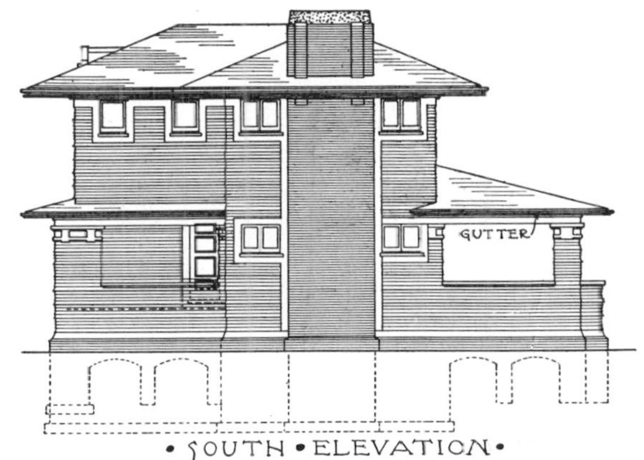

A Fine Type of Suburban Home

Tallmadge & Watson, Architects, Chicago, Illinois

THE plan of this house is interesting in the way the living room, hall, and dining room are arranged so as to form one big room and yet be sufficiently separated by posts and by the window and door arrangement. The inside finish of the main rooms is plain oak. Narrow weatherboarding mitered at the corners has been used on the outside and it looks exceedingly well. The boards, if stained instead of painted, should be turned rough side out. The house, which is the residence of Mr. Barrett Andrews, Oak Park, Illinois, was built in 1905 at a cost of $5,400.

The Simple Square Lines of This Cottage Harmonize with Its Admirable Setting of Shrubs and with the Forest Trees beyond

An Inexpensive Southern Cottage

Designed by Robert C. Spencer, Jr., Chicago, Illinois

THE design shows an attractive feature in the commodious living porch which, in the southern climate, is a very comfortable spot for the greater part of the year. The porch is connected by French windows to the large and open living room which, with its dining alcove and cozy corners, makes a cool and inviting interior arrangement. The exterior walls are covered with yellow pine "shiplap," left rough to stain. The ample overhang of the roof shelters the bedrooms and allows the windows to stand open, except during a driving rainstorm. This cottage could have been built in 1909 for about $2,000, itemized as follows: Masonry, $115; carpentry, lumber, and mill work, $1,220; sheet metal, $26; plastering, $240; painting, $92; glazing, $35; hardware, $43; plumbing, $220. Present prices would increase this estimate about twenty-five per cent.

PORCH 6'9" X 7'6"
ICE
KITCHEN 11'8" X 13'6"
SINK
COATS
PANTRY
RANGE
UP
DINING-ALCOVE
BOOKS
SEAT
LIVING-ROOM 15'0" X 32'9"
SEAT
BOOKS
ENTRANCE PORCH.
LIVING-PORCH 13'6" X 14'6"

First Floor Plan

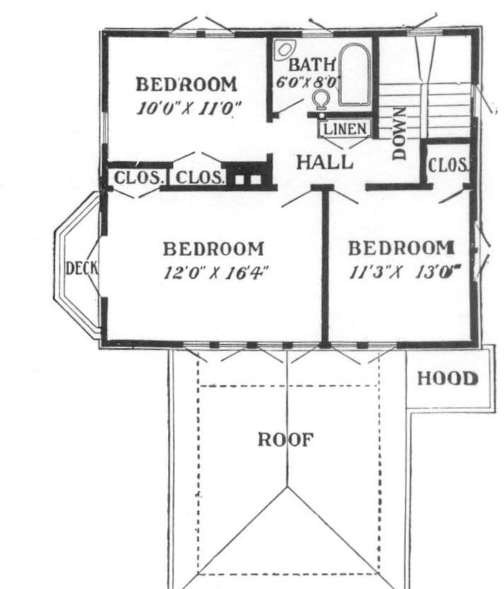

Second Floor Plan

•FIRST • FLOOR • PLAN •

A Delightful Low-Cost "Square" House

Vernon S. Watson, Architect, Chicago, Illinois

IT is very difficult to secure a house with attractive exterior and well-arranged plan at so low a cost as $2,000, but the architect accomplished this when he built this home for himself in 1909 at Oak Park, Illinois. The outside walls up to the window sills are covered with wide boards, and the joints are covered with narrow strips stained a soft brown. The upper part of the house to the second story window sills is covered with a narrow clapboarding, stained a moss-green color. Above this a frieze is formed of a cement stucco. The windows are leaded glass casements. There is no third story or attic, but the sewing room is large enough for the use of a servant.

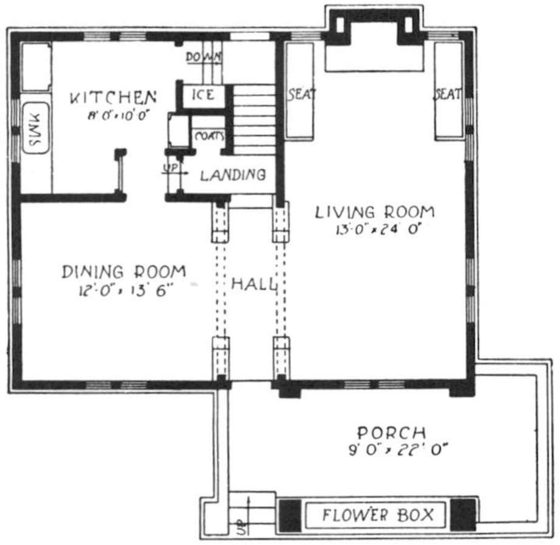

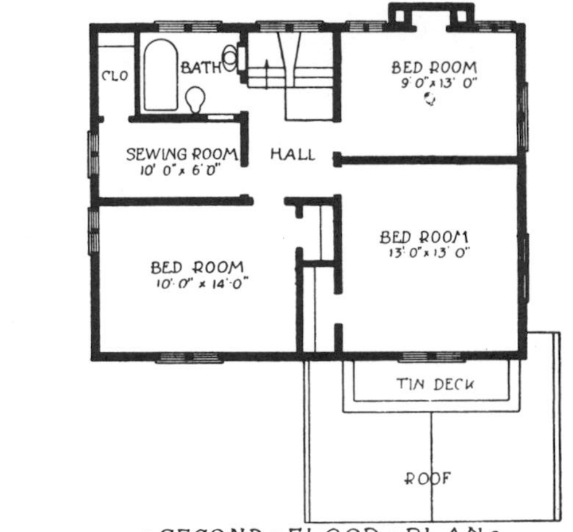

• SECOND • FLOOR • PLAN •

Reproduction of the Original Water-Color Sketch by the Architect

A Commodious-Looking Country Home

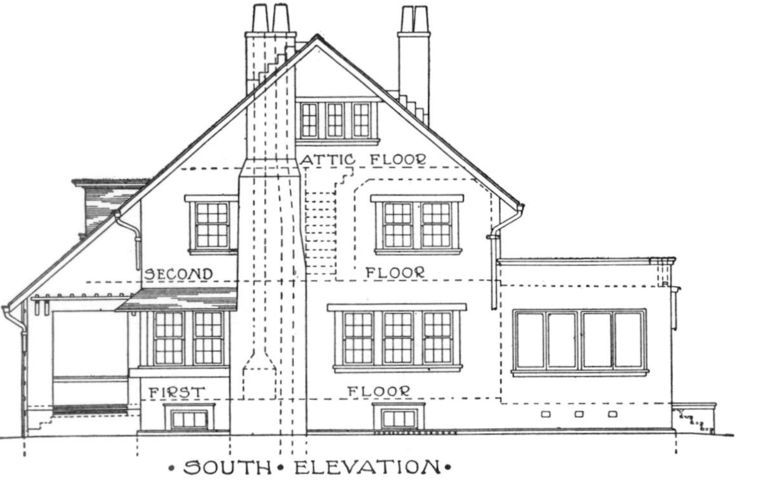

Lawrence Buck, Architect,
Chicago, Illinois

THE exterior walls of this house, the residence of Mr. Max H. Penwell, Pana, Illinois, are of frame, sheathed and felted and covered with 1 inch × 8 inch pine boards, rough side out. The roofs are covered with red cedar shingles. The interior finish is selected red birch throughout the main rooms of the first story. The finished floors are of red oak. The foundations are of brick plastered with Portland cement. For plans and sections see plate following.

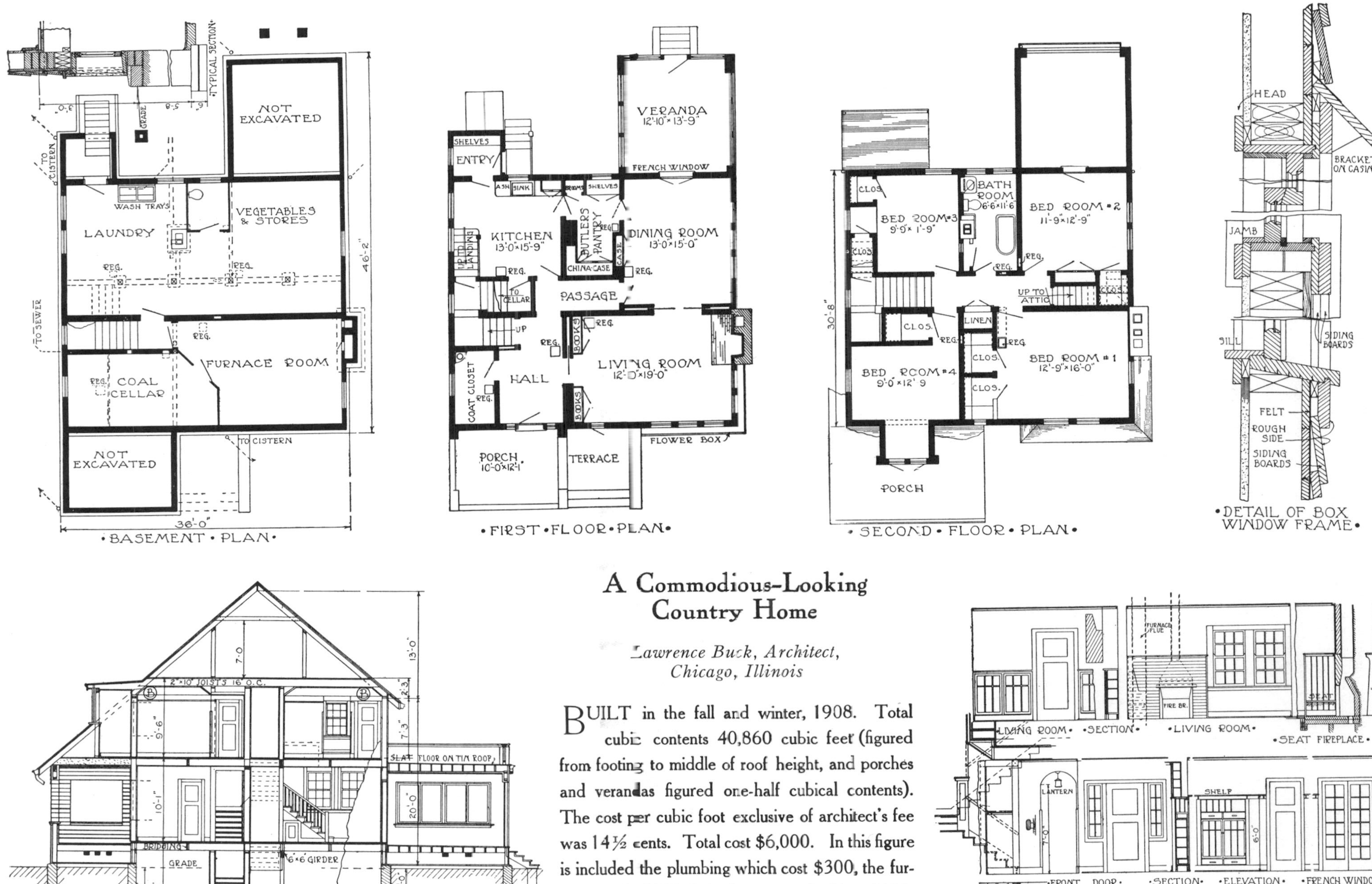

A Commodious-Looking Country Home

Lawrence Buck, Architect, Chicago, Illinois

BUILT in the fall and winter, 1908. Total cubic contents 40,860 cubic feet (figured from footing to middle of roof height, and porches and verandas figured one-half cubical contents). The cost per cubic foot exclusive of architect's fee was 14½ cents. Total cost $6,000. In this figure is included the plumbing which cost $300, the furnace work $200, light fixtures and wiring $115. For exterior and elevations, see plate preceding.

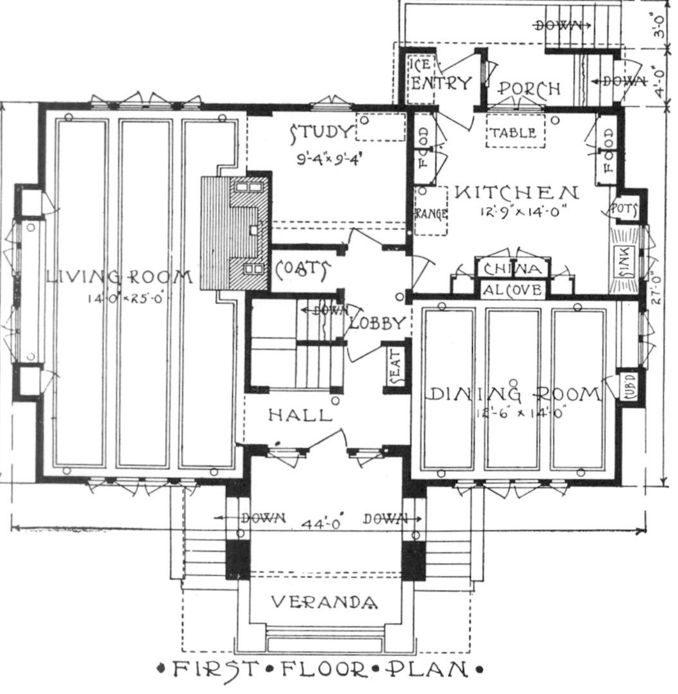

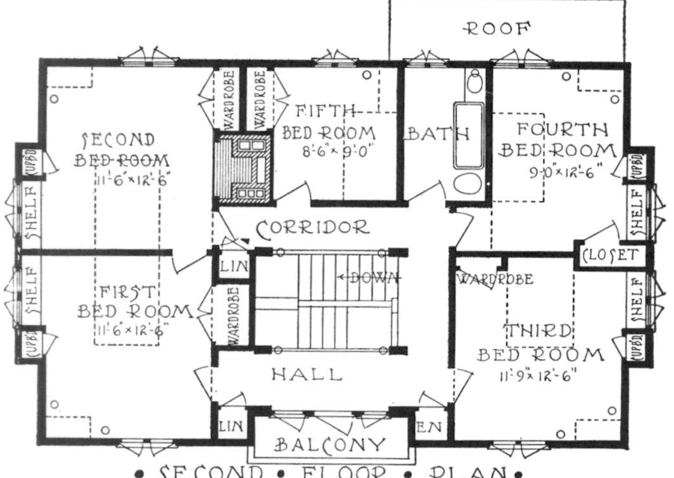

A Frame and Stucco Country House

Charles E. White, Jr., Architect, Chicago, Illinois

THIS simple yet artistic dwelling has a frame exterior with stucco on wood lath and a shingle roof. The interior design is along the same simple lines as shown in the exterior view, the woodwork being of southern pine. The house faces south. It is the home of Mr. Walter Gerts, River Forest, Illinois, and was built in 1905 at a cost of $5,500.

PANTRY
PORCH
KITCHEN 10'-9"×11'-6"
DINING ROOM 11'-9"×14'-3"
UP
DOWN
HALL
LIVING ROOM 13'-0"×23'-9"
PORCH

• FIRST • STORY •

The Sholes House in River Forest, Illinois, Showing Commodious Living Porch

An Effective Suburban Home of Moderate Cost

Henry K. Holsman, Architect, Chicago, Illinois

THE front entrance faces east, thus giving the living porch the most desirable exposure, the south.

The exterior walls in the lower story are covered with wide and narrow boards alternating, while from the second story windows to the roof they are finished with stucco. The windows are made wide and generous, in good proportion to the mass of the building. In this type of plan every room has good cross ventilation by having windows on both sides of the rooms. The interior is finished in hardwood. Built in 1906 for about $3,500.

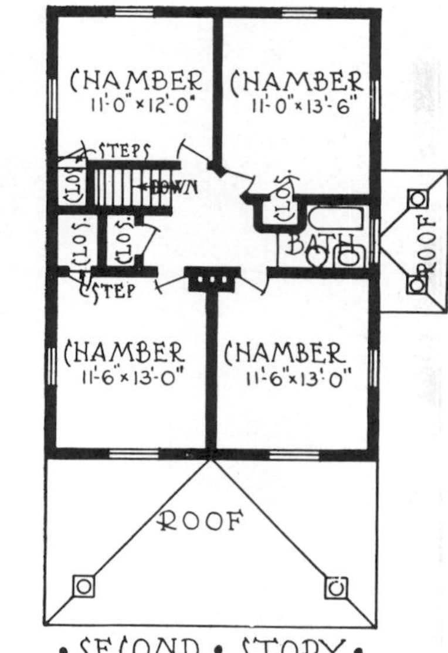

• SECOND • STORY •

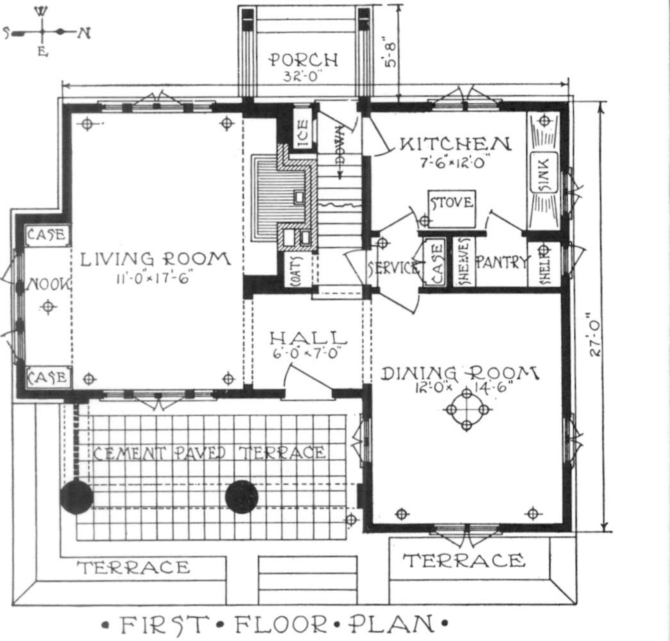

•FIRST•FLOOR•PLAN•

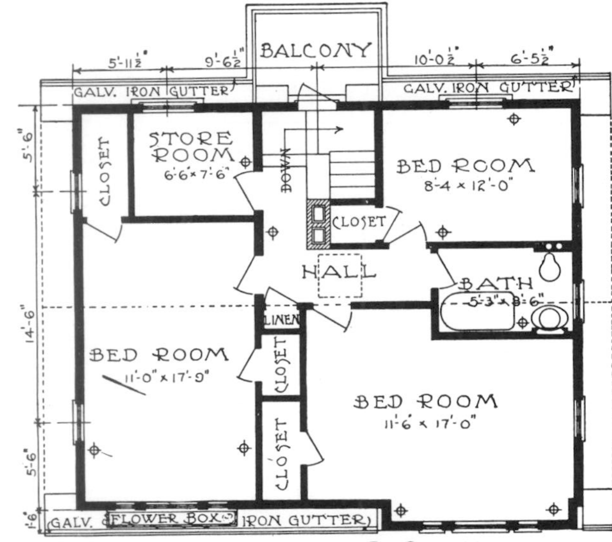

•SECOND•FLOOR•PLAN•

A Frame and Shingle Dwelling of Unusual and Effective Design

Tallmadge & Watson, Architects, Chicago, Illinois

THE house, which is the residence of Mr. Whitney T. Lovell, Oak Park, Illinois, shows an interesting shingle treatment. The round high gable, the massive cement columns, and the roof sweeping down to the first story form a good contrast. The interior is trimmed in plain birch with mouse-grey finish. The plan is compact and yet very roomy. The house was built in 1906 and cost $4,200.

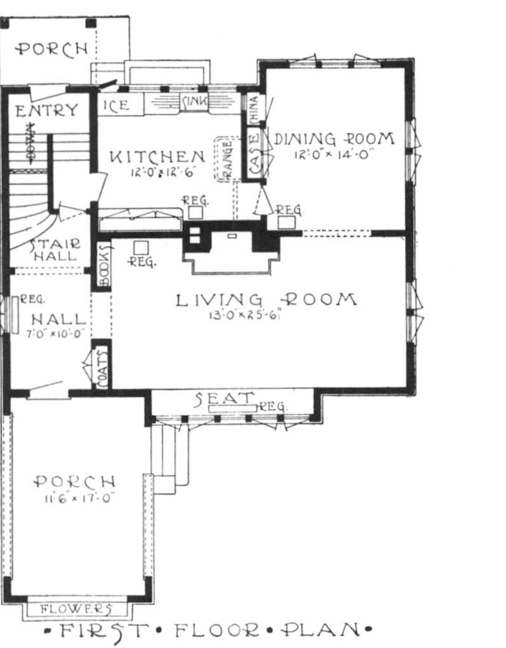

•FIRST • FLOOR • PLAN•

DECK
BATH
CLOSET
BED ROOM 12'-0"x13'-0"
HALL
LINEN
BED ROOM 11'-6"x12'-0"
BED ROOM 14'-0"x22'-0"
HOOD
ROOF
N E W S

•SECOND • FLOOR • PLAN•

An Inexpensive Suburban Home

Spencer & Powers, Architects,
Chicago, Illinois

THIS is an excellent type of small family house in plan as well as in exterior treatment. The lower portion of the walls is covered with rough boards stained brown. The absence of corner boards gives the house a more solid looking effect. The second story portion, including the underside of roof, is covered with grey plaster. The windows are casements painted white. The whole color scheme is very harmonious with the surrounding trees. The interior finish is oak with stain and wax finish in hall, living room, and dining room; yellow pine in kitchen portion, and poplar painted in bedrooms. The house is located in River Forest, Illinois, and was built for Mr. Edward S. Bristol in 1908 at a cost of $5,000—not including architects' fees.

Plaster and Shingle House at Kenilworth, Illinois

Cement Plaster House at Kenilworth, Illinois, with Exquisite Setting of Foliage

Four Country Houses Showing Different Exterior Treatment

THE question of the material to be used for the exterior of a house is dependent upon the local materials at hand and on the surroundings. Perfect harmony with the setting gives the impression of the house having grown out of the soil. Judicious planting of shrubs and the proper placing of the house among the trees contributes greatly to this end.

Interesting Treatment with Narrow Clapboards and White Trimmings on a Suburban House

Modest Little Country House Near Chicago, Shingled All Over with Trimmings Painted Ivory White

Brick and Stucco Dwelling with Decided Colonial Aspect

Hewitt & Emerson, Architects, Peoria, Illinois

FIRST FLOOR PLAN

THE white trim, the green blinds, and the column treatment of entrance and porch lend a colonial atmosphere to the design. The first story is of brick veneer and the second story, which is of stucco, overhangs the first. The staircase is made a feature of the living room. The house faces east. It was built for Mr. Frank T. Miller, Peoria, in 1908, and cost about $8,500, including plumbing and heating.

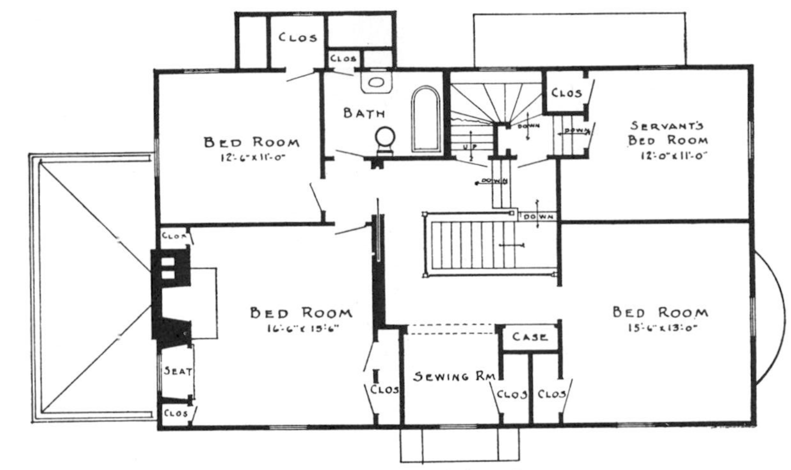

SECOND FLOOR PLAN

The Overhanging Eaves Coupled with the Straight Lines Give an Impression of Extreme Breadth. The Interior Arrangement of the First Floor Is Very Well Worked Out

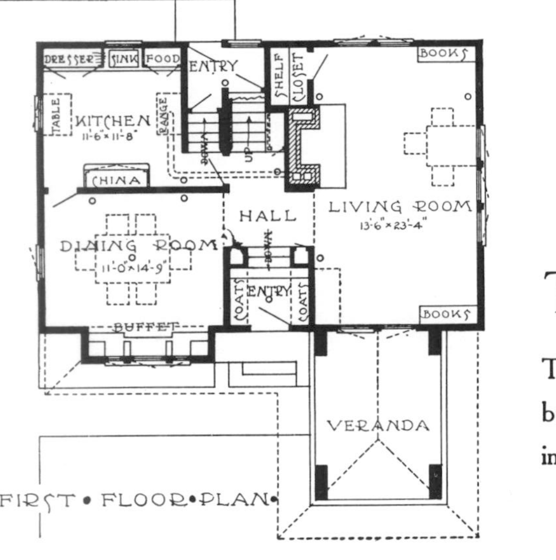

A Cement Plaster House, Almost Severe in Its Simplicity

Charles E. White, Jr., Architect, Chicago, Illinois

THE outside walls are covered with cement plaster, treated in big broad surfaces with a base of wide wood boards. The roofs are covered with shingles. The interior is finished in southern pine. A rather unique arrangement of the buffet in the dining room is shown on the first floor plan. This house was built in 1905 for Mrs. C. E. Simmons, Oak Park, Illinois, at a cost of $5,000.

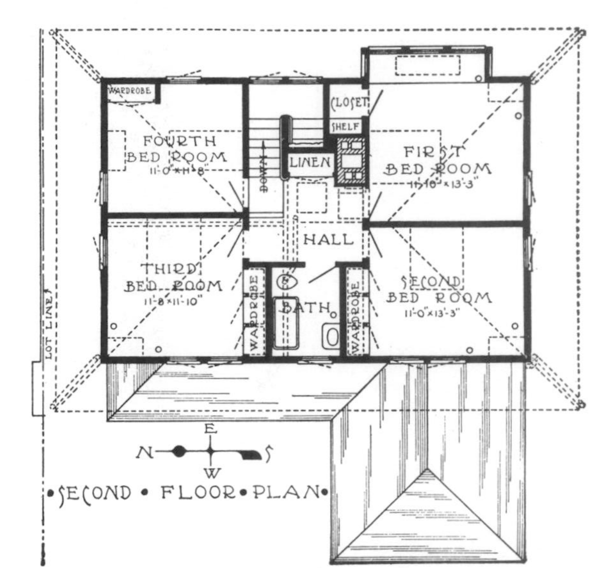

PLATE 32

The Oldfield Bungalow, Oak Park, Illinois. An Attractive Dwelling with an Interesting Treatment of Porch Rail

An Unpretentious, but Very Homelike Cottage in Oak Park, Illinois. A Few Shrubs Would Help Bring Out the Charm

This Stucco House Is Given a Most Delightful Accent by the Small Entrance Porch with Its Classical Columns. Residence of A. M. Tinsman, Wilmette, Illinois. *Arthur G. Brown, Architect, Chicago, Illinois.*

Cement Plaster Houses

THESE houses are notable for the almost total elimination of wood on the exterior, most of the windows having only plaster jambs, "stucco treated." Such broad surfaces must be put on very carefully to avoid cracks in the plaster.

A Well-Designed Cottage in Wilmette, Illinois, with Window Frames and Trim of Unplaned Lumber, Stained a Rich Brown

A Suburban House of Moderate Cost in Oak Park, Illinois. The Introduction of the Two Curved Gables in the Front Lends an Odd Interest to the Simple Design

• FIRST • FLOOR • PLAN •

• SECOND • FLOOR • PLAN •

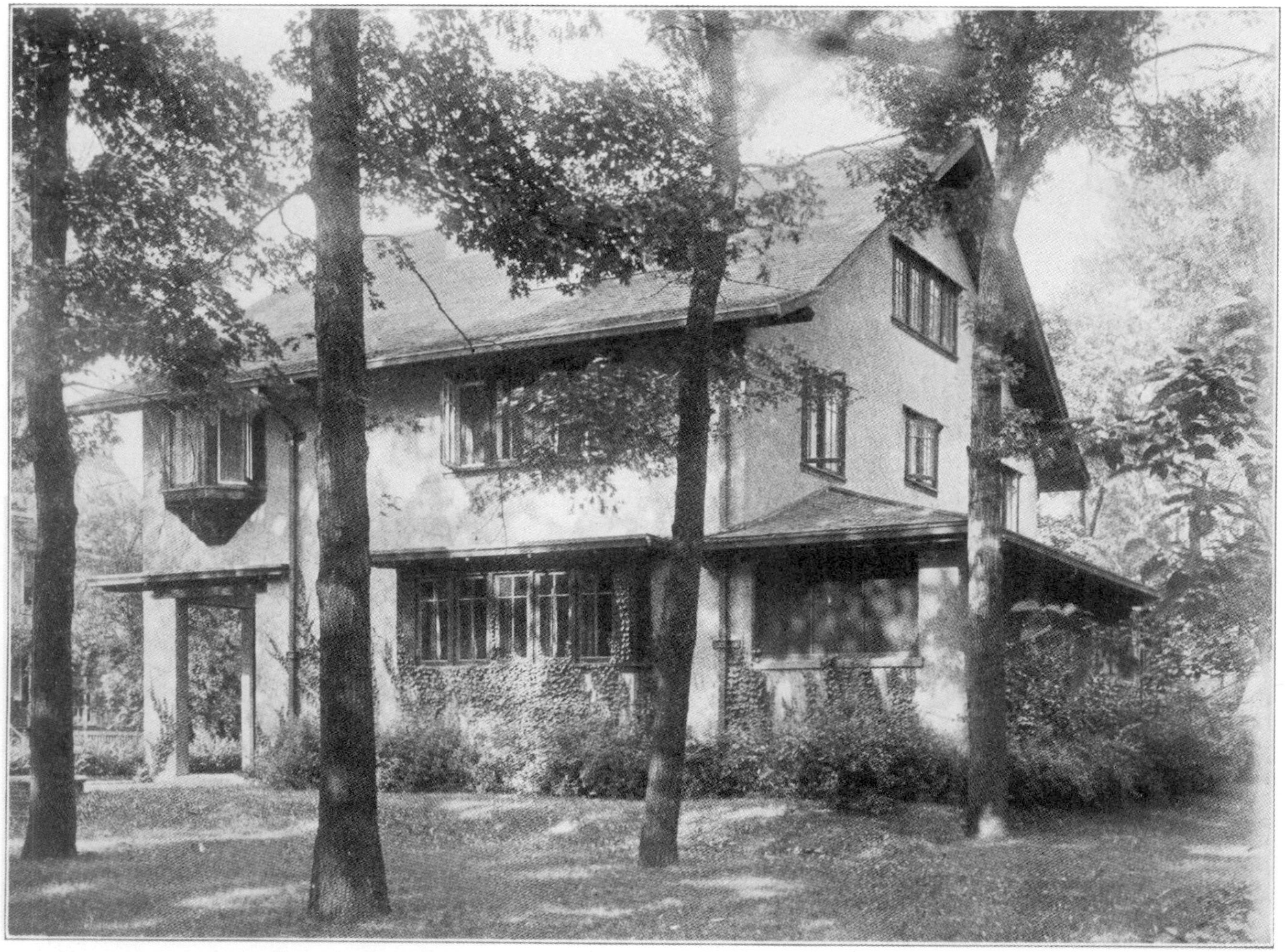

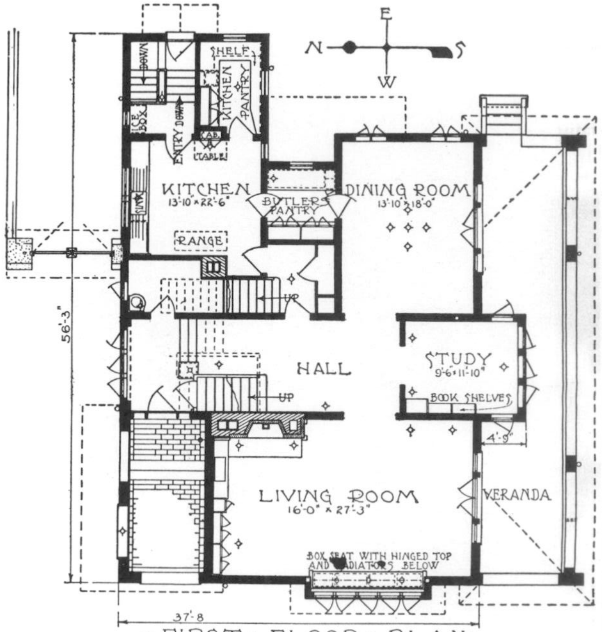

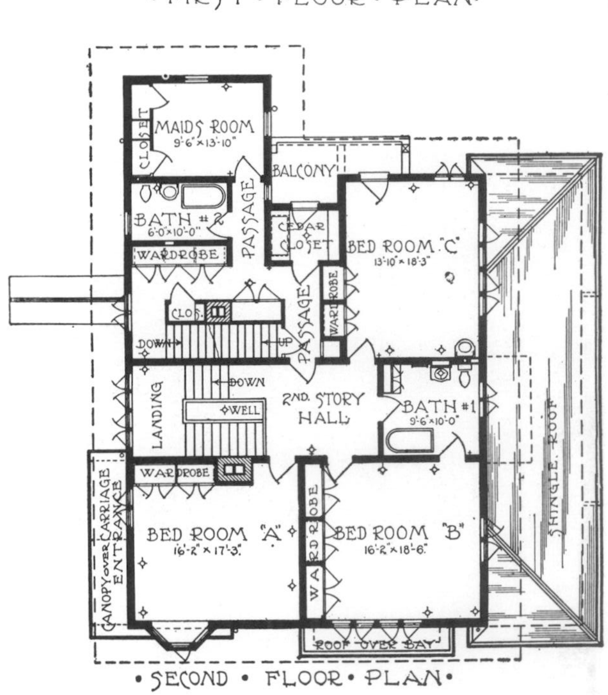

A Well-Planned Cement Plaster House of Dignified Character

Lawrence Buck, Architect, Chicago, Illinois

THIS cement plaster house was built in 1908 and is the residence of Mr. E. H. Ehrman, Oak Park, Illinois. Its principal charm lies in the design and arrangement of the windows. Note how the ledge over the entrance, the cornice of the living room windows, and the cornice over the porch are made to line up. The house is kept low on the ground, and this effect is emphasized by having the steps inside the entrance porch. Casement windows have been used throughout except in the service portion. The interior finish in the main rooms is oak. The dining room has a plain paneled wainscot. Cost $13,000.

A Modern Country Home in Oak Park, Illinois. *W. A. Purcell, Architect, Minneapolis, Minnesota*

A House in Kenilworth, Illinois, of Dignified Exterior, Suggestive of Comfort and Breadth Within
Edgar O. Blake, Architect, Evanston, Illinois

A Modest House in Oak Park, Illinois. A Novel Effect Is Obtained by Carrying the Spindles of the Porch Railing to the Grade

Four Suburban Homes in the Vicinity of Chicago, Illinois

THE predominating exterior treatment in these houses is plaster with a variation of brick in the first story of the upper left, half timber in the second story of the one opposite, and local field stones close to the ground in the house at the lower right. They illustrate very clearly the charming variety which is possible in the modern suburban home.

A Country House in Which Local Field Stones Have Been Used to Good Advantage

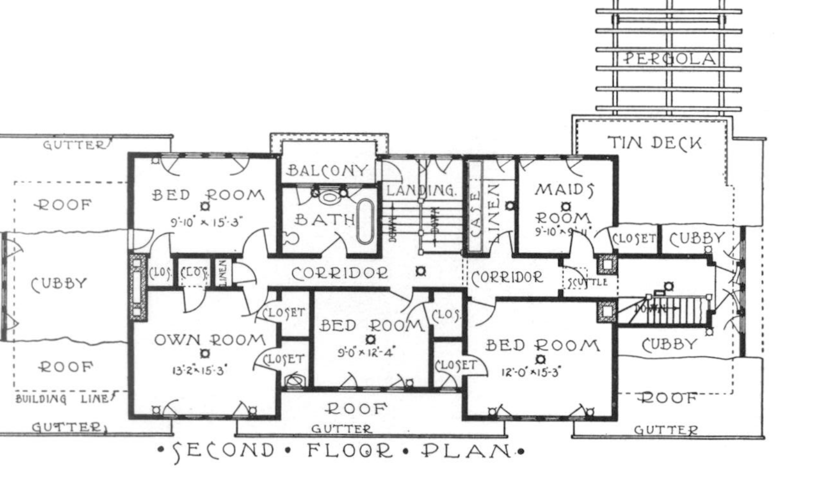

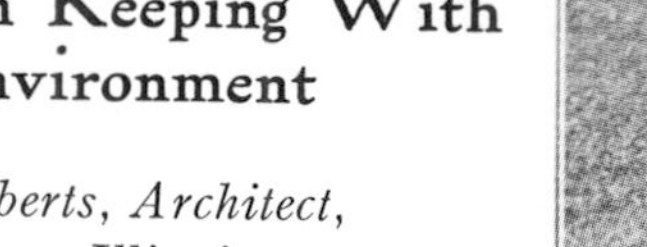

A Design in Keeping With Its Environment

E. E. Roberts, Architect, Chicago, Illinois

Front View Showing Fine Foliage Setting and Broad Expanse of Lawn

Rear View Showing Trees on Lake Shore

THIS house, the residence of Mr. Byron Williams, Glen Ellyn, Illinois, is an interesting example of the adaptation of the plan to the site. The living room, porch, dining room, and hall run through the house, giving them the southern exposure (front) and also a view of the small lake on the shore of which the house is built. The outside walls are of frame, the wood lath being covered with a cement plaster. The interior trim is oak in the principal rooms on the first floor and birch and yellow pine elsewhere. The house was built in 1907 and cost about $8,000.

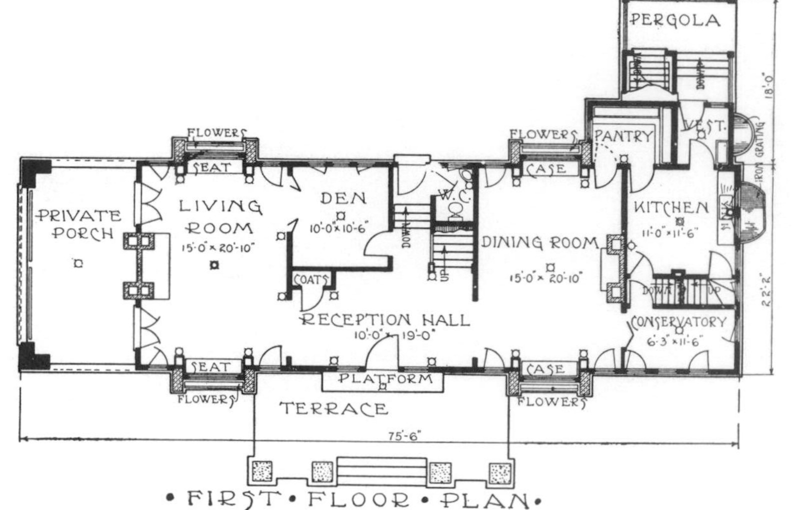

Colonial Hall in Mr. Meacham's House

Two Effective Stucco Houses

Thornton Herr,
Architect,
Chicago, Illinois

Concrete and Cement Plaster House of Mr. Chas. S. Meacham, Oak Park, Illinois

THE upper house has a decided colonial feeling, especially in the interior. The large porch is made a part of the garden by having the floor close to the ground and by having no porch railing. The smaller house has a homelike quality partly due to the way the roof is carried down, which ties together the porch and the living room window.

An Inexpensive Farmhouse of Cement Plaster, Oak Park, Illinois

Living Room and Fireplace, with Dining Room Shown in the Background, in the Oak Park Farmhouse

Country Home of Mr. Wm. Grenshaw at Glen Ellyn, Illinois. The Owner Was His Own Architect

Farmhouse at Natoma Farm, Hinsdale, Illinois

Farmhouse Near Toledo, Ohio

Colonial Farmhouses

THE country house in America is being developed more and more and in many of them one will find the feeling of the old colonial Southern homes, a style which is well adapted to a house having abundant space around it to give the colonial lines a dignified setting.

Colonial Farmhouse in the Elgin Dairy District

Four Simple Comfortable Homes

Designed by Arthur T. Remick

An Excellent Example of the Old-Fashioned Homestead

Designed by Coolidge & Carlson

A Compact Design Giving Much Room in Small Compass

With Its White Clapboard Exterior, Green Blinds, and Roomy Porch, This House Looks Very Homelike

A Modern Design with Brick Walls and Gambrel Roof, Which Are Effectively Worked Out

A Compact Home in a Small City

Lawrence Buck, Architect, Chicago, Illinois

THIS house, the residence of Mr. Walter Boyle, Rockford, Illinois, is of frame with expanded metal lath and a prepared cement plaster on the outside. The porch in front of the house is especially attractive and shows an unusual treatment in the combination of the arches on the side, the roof and flower box at second story windows, all worked together in a harmonious whole. The house was built in 1908 and cost $5,500. For plans, elevations, and sections, see two plates following.

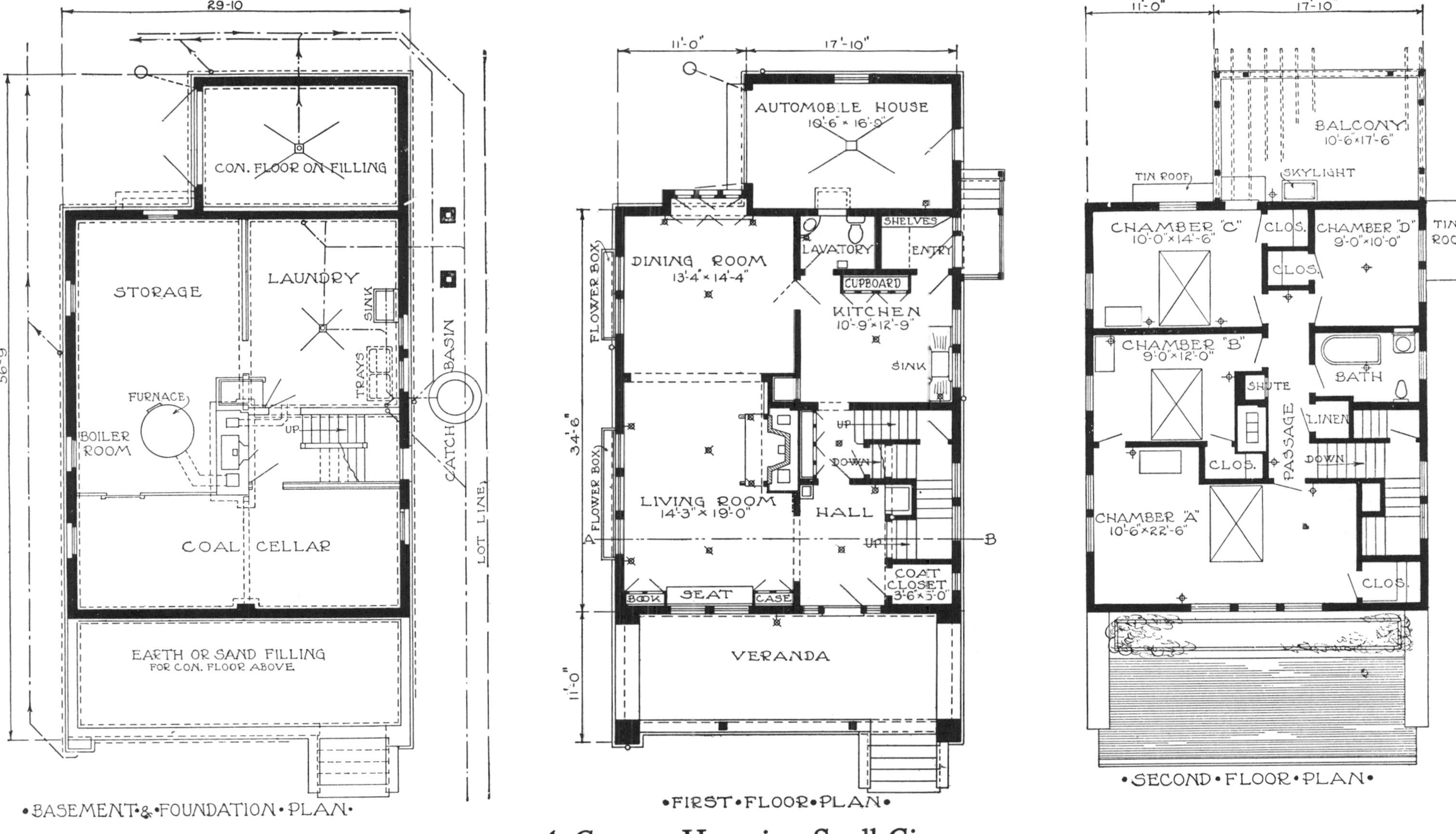

A Compact Home in a Small City

Lawrence Buck, Architect,
Chicago, Illinois

THIS plan shows a very economical way of combining the garage with the house. This combination not only saves money but leaves the entire back yard for planting and laundry yard. The living and dining room are combined into one large room, the line of division being marked by an arched opening. For exterior, elevations, and section, see plates preceding and following.

•EAST•ELEVATION•

•SOUTH•ELEVATION•

A Compact Home in a Small City

Lawrence Buck, Architect, Chicago, Illinois

THE grouping and proportions of all openings are very simple and effective. Small hoods are placed over the windows for shedding the water. The roof of the automobile house is flat and is utilized as a balcony with an open timber roof above. This makes an admirable porch for summer time, being on the west side of the house and affording a fine view of the garden. For exterior and plans, see two plates preceding.

ATTIC FLOOR

SECOND FLOOR

FIRST FLOOR

BASEMENT FLOOR

8'-6"

10'-3"

8'-6"

•NORTH•ELEVATION•

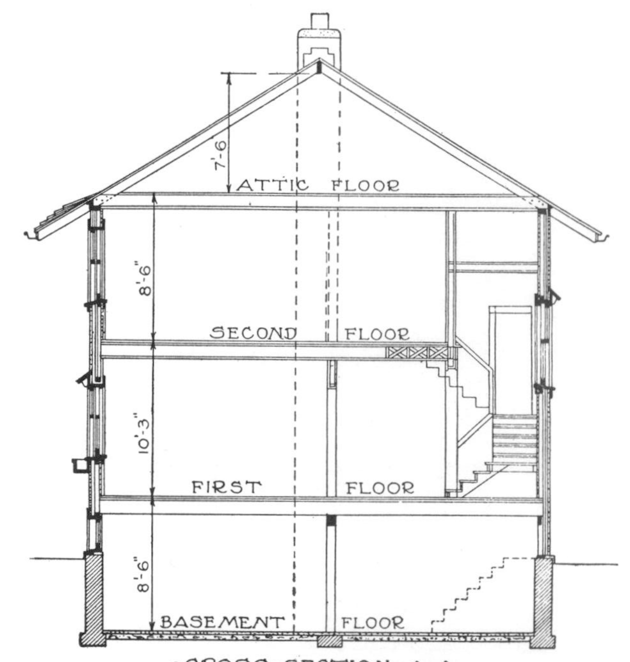

•CROSS•SECTION•A-A•

Four Typical Old-Fashioned Homes

Designed by George E. Strout

The Log Exterior and Broad Porch Give a Substantial Air to This House

Designed by J. J. Blick

Except for the Long Pergola the Atmosphere of This Home Is Distinctly Colonial

Designed by Hunt & Grey

The Low Effect of the Gambrel Roof Is Very Typical

Designed by Mellor & Meigs

An Old-Fashioned House, Almost Church-like in Character. Built of Pennsylvania Field Stone

Contributed by Virginia Stein

This Frame and Plaster Dwelling Shows Considerable Individuality with Simple Lines. The Roof Treatment and Pergola Are Very Effective

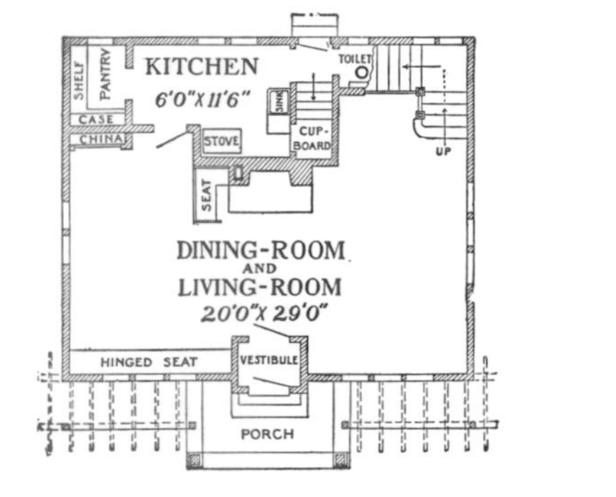

First Floor Plan

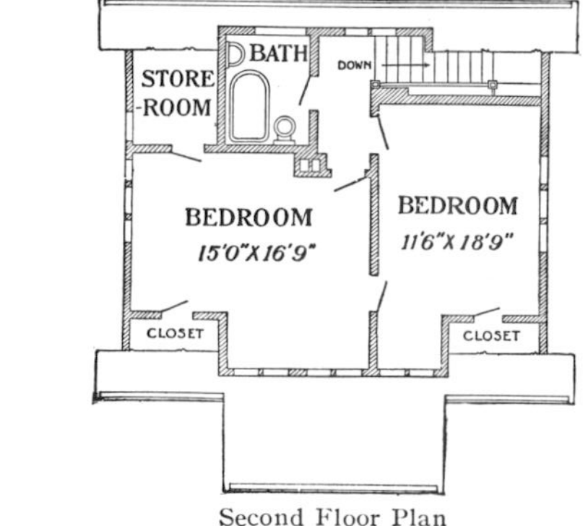

Second Floor Plan

Contributed by Mahlon J. Bye

The Owner of This House Was the Architect. The Living Porch and Sloping Lawn Make the Rear as Attractive as the Front

First Floor Plan

Second Floor Plan

Two-Story Country Houses of Moderate Cost

THE grey stucco exterior with dull green shingles makes a charming effect. As this house was built for two city girls, their idea of having a fine large combination living and dining room is a good one, the arrangement lending itself admirably to light housekeeping. The same simplicity has been carried out on the interior as on the exterior, the materials being of good quality, but of modest design. Cost $2,500.

THE shingled exterior and the simple gables give a very homelike appearance. The interior arrangement is compact and convenient, the living room and porch giving a very sizable suite and the second floor showing a surprise in four bedrooms, store-room, and bath. The house is furnace heated, piped for gas, and equipped with modern plumbing. Cost $3,400.

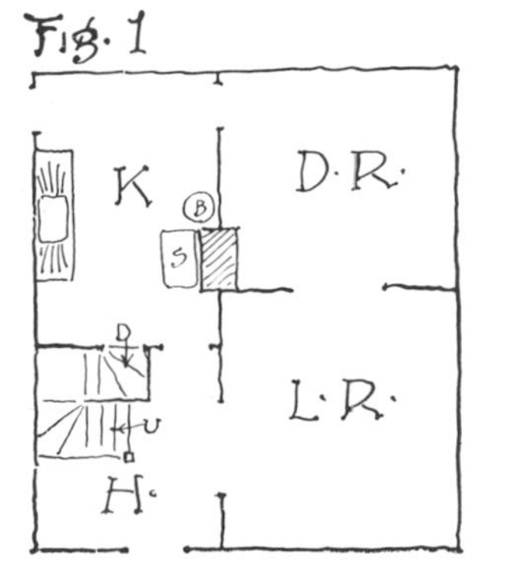

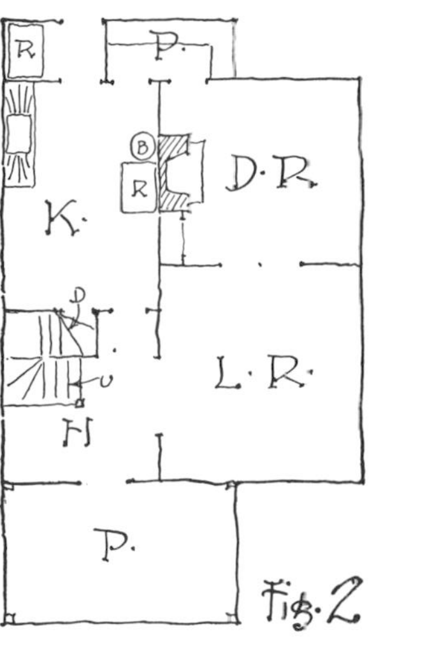

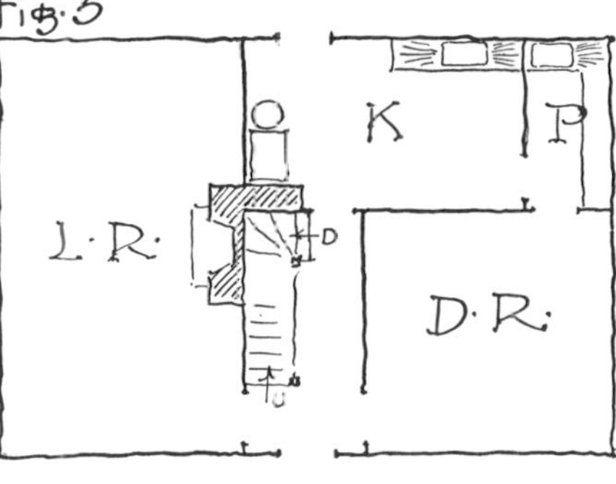

The Uniformity of Modern Floor Plans

THE first question confronting a prospective home builder is how many rooms are there to be and how shall they be arranged. After this question has been decided, the next one is: How shall the rooms be grouped in order to give the most economical arrangement? An important consideration is to have the various rooms arranged in such a way that they have the best possible exposure as far as light and air and views are concerned. It will be found that most house plans can be reduced to a very few types. These six sketch plans illustrate the first floor plans of houses, starting with a very simple arrangement with but one staircase to a plan having the elements necessary for a large house. Fig. 1 is the type of the average low cost house. Fig. 2 has a pantry, ice box, alcove, and front yard added. Fig. 3 has a central hall arrangement, with the chimney so arranged that it will serve for the furnace flue, kitchen flue, and dining room fireplace. Fig. 4 has two chimneys and an extra room for a den in the rear. Fig. 5 has an ell extension to give more space to the pantry and kitchen. Fig. 6 gives four large rooms in a square plan. Only after having given ample thought to the arrangement of the plan, can the question of exterior "looks" be successfully considered.

Fireplace Built of Tapestry. Brick and Tile Inlay at Top
Lawrence Buck, Architect, Chicago, Illinois

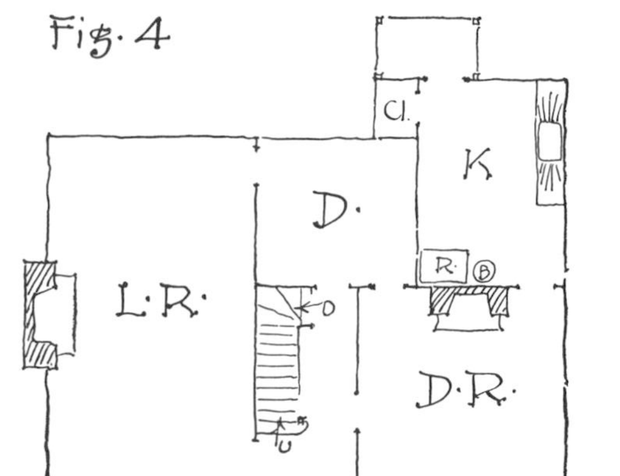

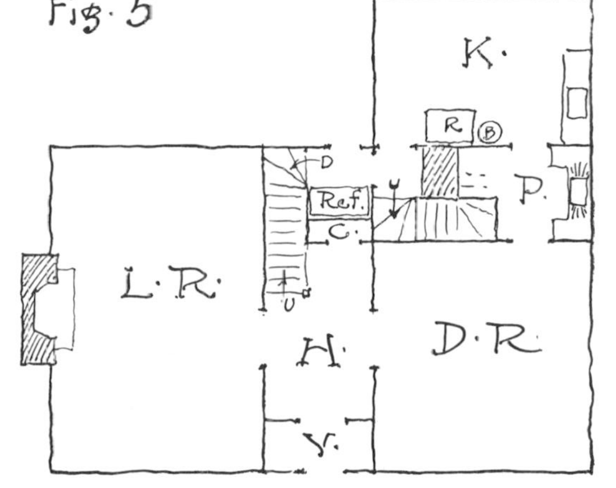

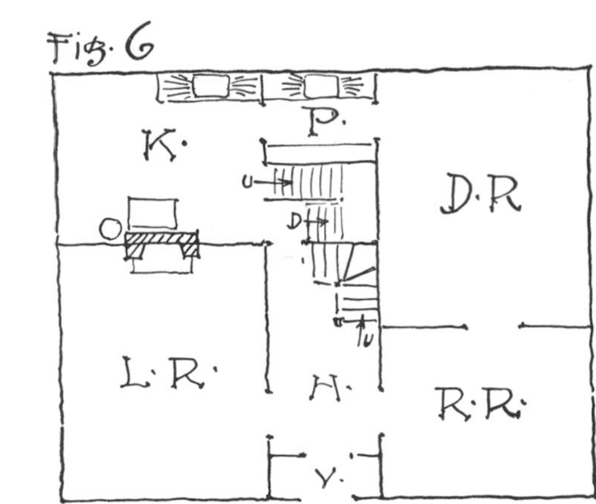

Colonial Type of House with Hip-Roof. This May Be Executed in Wood, Plaster, or Brick

This Design Has the Feeling of an English Country House of Brick or Plaster, with Small Windows

First Floor Plan

A Colonial Design with Gable Ends—Brick Material

Studies of Different Exterior Treatments of the Same Plan

THESE pen and ink sketches by Lawrence Buck, Architect, Chicago, Illinois, show the possibilities of variation in the exterior style of the house after the plan has been decided upon. The rough studies enable the architect to find out for himself what type of exterior design will best suit the location and also to ascertain the preference of the client for different types of houses.

A Plaster or Brick Design. The Hip-Roof Combined with the Arches Gives It an Italian Feeling

An English Type of House. Plaster or Brick Would Be Suitable Materials for This Design

View of the Blount Bungalow Showing Street Front. The Commodious Screen Veranda Adds Much to the Comfort of the Home.

A Simple Country Home of the Bungalow Type

Walter Burley Griffin, Architect, Chicago, Illinois

THIS house, the residence of Mr. R. L. Blount, Tracy, Illinois, is set close to the ground, the wood base and horizontal lines helping this effect. The exterior stucco work is a natural grey cement color; the woodwork is stained an olive green. The shingles are without stain and are left to weather naturally. For plans and further elevations, see plate following.

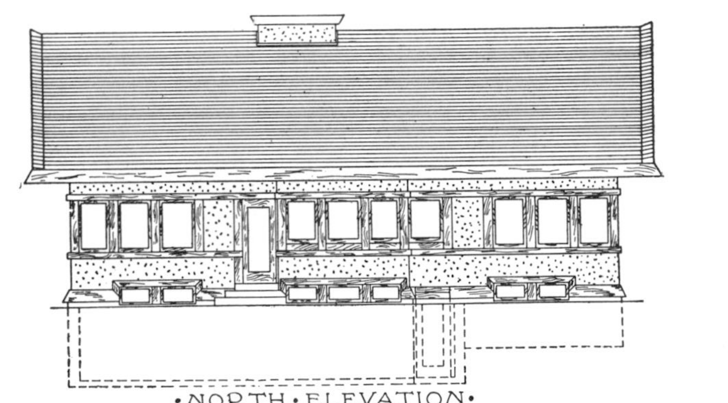

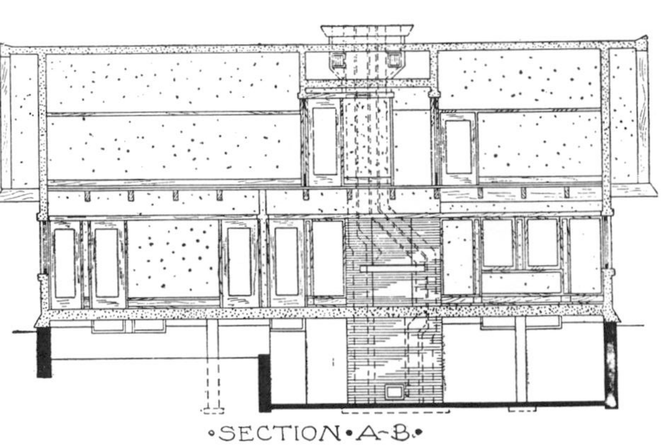

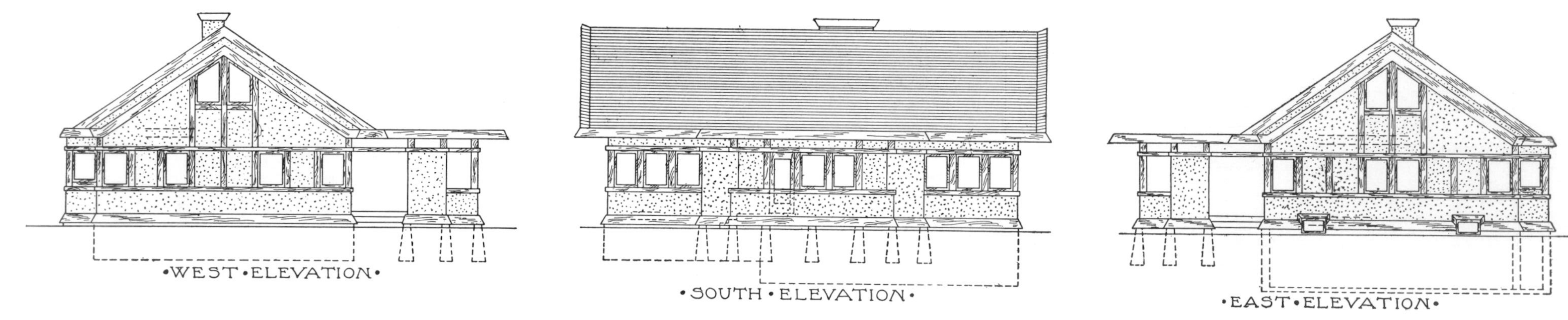

A Simple Country Home of the Bungalow Type

Walter Burley Griffin, Architect, Chicago, Illinois

THE plan is simple in outline, in order to reduce the cost as much as possible. Casement windows have been used throughout. The grouping of the windows at the corners is noticeable, giving the maximum light and air. The usual downspouts have been dispensed with, the water dropping into rainbasins placed underneath openings in the gutters. The interior trim is oak in the main rooms and pine in the service portion. The ceiling beams are left exposed thus giving greater height to the rooms. The house was built in 1909 and cost $4,000. For photograph of exterior and further elevations, see plate preceding.

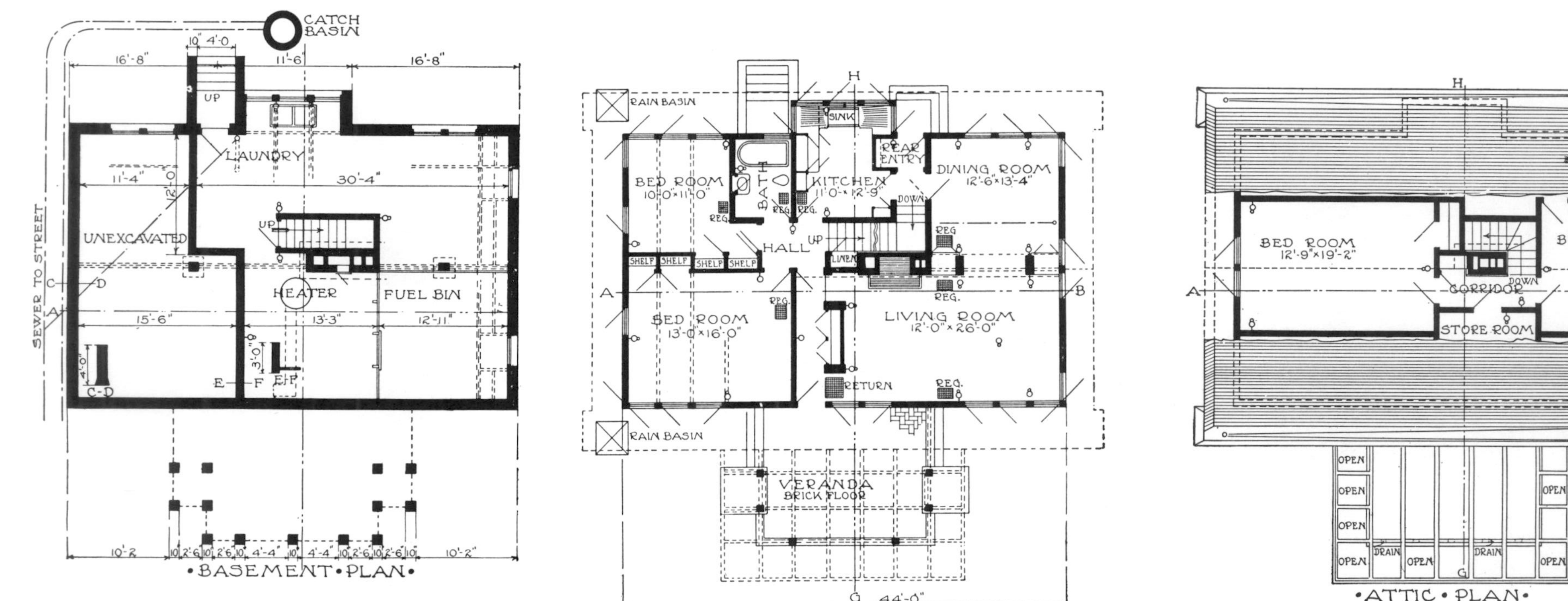

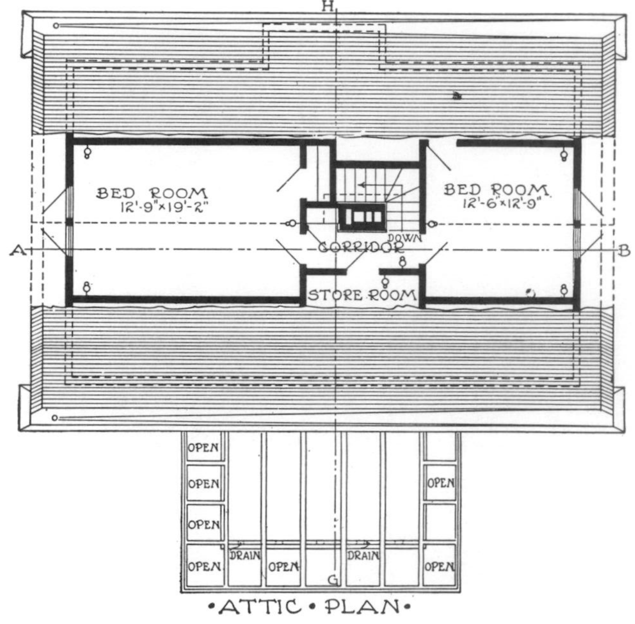

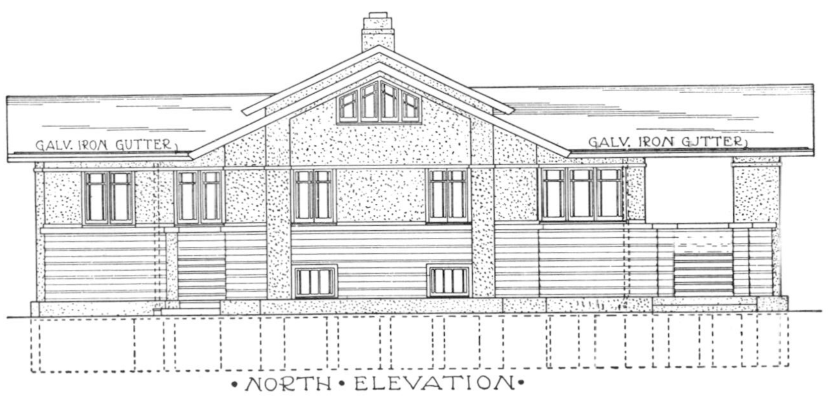

• NORTH • ELEVATION •

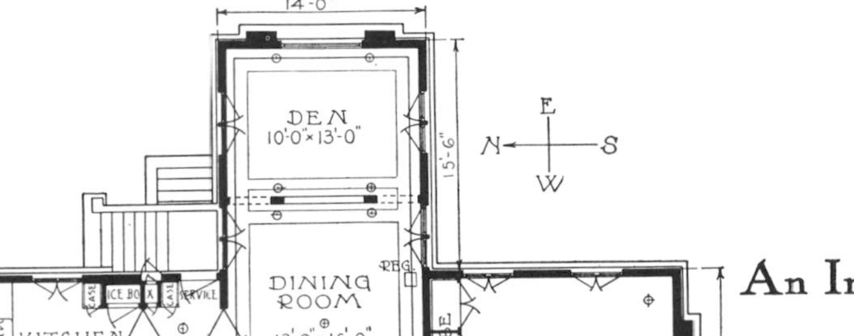
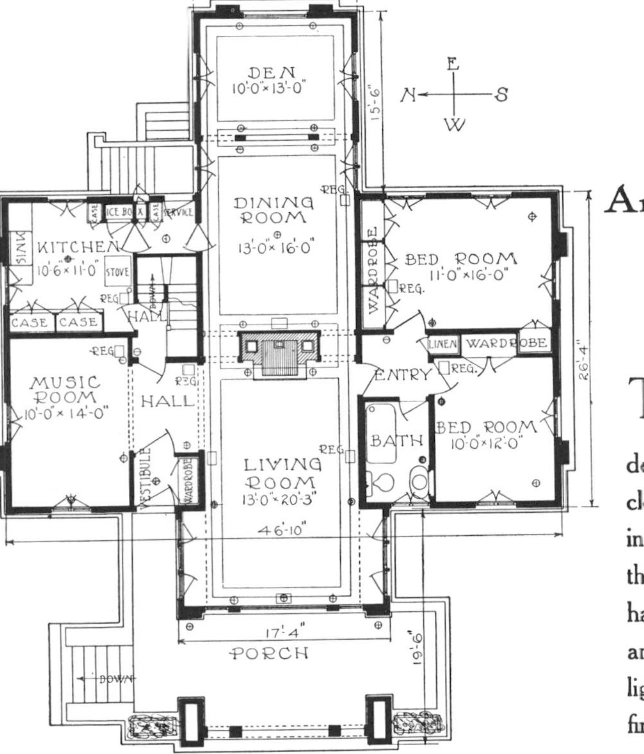

FIRST • FLOOR • PLAN •

An Interesting Suburban Home with Garage in the Basement

Tallmadge & Watson, Architects
Chicago, Illinois

THIS bungalow, which is the residence of Mr. T. S. Estabrook, Oak Park, Illinois, is a refreshing departure from stereotyped designs. An unusual and cleverly-handled feature is the placing of the garage in the basement, the floor of the garage being on the basement floor level. The exterior shows a happy combination of shingles in the lower portion and plaster above. The porch does not cut off the light from the main rooms. The interior has sand-finished walls and flat trim. The cost of this house was about $7,000.

Front View Showing Entrance and Living Porch

Rear View Showing Garage Entrance

The Lower Part of This House is Covered with Boards Put on Vertically, Wide and Narrow Boards Alternating; the Upper Part Is Covered with Shingles. It Cost about $800

Five Rooms and Bath Are in This Shingle House. The Living Room Has a Brick Fireplace and the Woodwork Is of Panel Finish. It Cost $1,200

This Attractive Tent House Has Two Rooms and Shower Bath. It is Exceptionally Well Built and Cost $300

A Compact Small House Containing Four Rooms and Bath. It was Designed by the Owner and Cost $800

Four Small Houses Showing the Value of Well-Placed Foliage

East Side of House, Showing Veranda. One Side of Living Room Faces This Veranda, the Other Looks Out on the Courtyard

North Side of House Showing Entrance and Drive. The Basement Walls are Visible Through the Shrubbery on the West Side

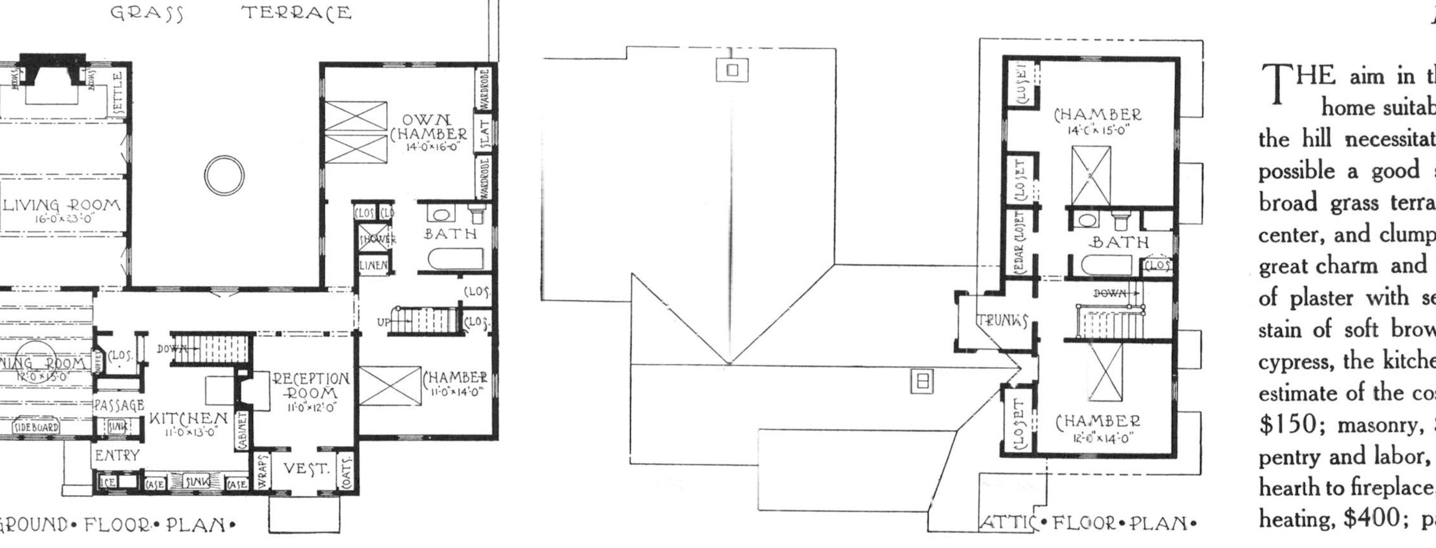

A Concrete Bungalow of Moderate Cost

A. G. Richardson, Architect,
Boston, Massachusetts

THE aim in this home was to provide an all-the-year home suitable to its environment. The deep slant of the hill necessitated an irregularity of contour, but made possible a good sized cellar beneath the west wing. A broad grass terrace, the courtyard with a fountain in the center, and clumps of shrubbery judiciously placed give a great charm and quaintness to the place. The exterior is of plaster with selected cypress trim treated with an oil stain of soft brown color. The main rooms are finished in cypress, the kitchen in white enamel paint. Following is an estimate of the cost of the bungalow complete: Excavation, $150; masonry, $300; timber and mill work, $940; carpentry and labor, $1,200; chimney, including herringbone hearth to fireplace, $200; plastering, $500; plumbing, $425; heating, $400; painting and staining, $185; total, $4,300.

This Delightfully Original House Has an Individuality All Its Own

GARDEN
POOL
MAID'S ROOM
SCREEN PORCH
KITCHEN 10'6"X11'0"
DOWN
UP
DINING-ROOM 12'0"X15'0"
LIVING PORCH
SEAT
LIVING-ROOM 15'0"X22'0"
HALL
BED-ROOM 10'6"X10'6"
SEAT
CLOS
BATH
ENTRANCE PORCH
BEDROOM 11'0" X 16'6"
CLOS
CLOS

First Floor Plan

Second Floor Plan

The Dining Room Is Indicative of the Good Taste Displayed Throughout the House

Country House with a Sleeping Porch

Designed by George A. Clark
Photographs by F. W. Martin

THE starting point of this country house was the big sleeping porch in the second story, and the rest of the design, both inside and out, was planned to harmonize with this feature. On three sides the porch is open, except that the second story wall is carried up to a height of about three feet above the floor level. During the day, in warm weather, when the cots have been converted into couches, there is no pleasanter spot in the whole house; in fact, it makes an admirable roof-garden. For further views, see plate following.

View Showing Living Porch and Formal Garden From Side of the House

Country House with a Sleeping Porch

Designed by George A. Clark
Photographs by F. W. Martin

A Corner of the Sleeping Porch

A DISTINCTIVE outdoor feature of this house is a small formal garden in the rear partly inclosed with a pergola and containing in the center a miniature fountain and pool. The dining room overlooks this attractive spot, where the well-kept walks are bordered with beds of flowers and the simple pergola is green with climbing vines. The living porch is so placed that it faces the little garden instead of an uninteresting roadway, as is so often the case. A house such as this offers many good suggestions to those who contemplate building and, considering the number of rooms, it can be duplicated for quite a moderate sum. For front view and plans, see plate preceding.

A Glimpse of the Formal Garden

Designed by William Cooper

Four-Room Bungalow with an Abundance of Light and Ventilation. The Windows Are Very Attractively Grouped. This House Cost about $1,200

Low-Cost Bungalows

Contributed by
Helen Lukens Gaut,
Pasadena, California

Designed by Mrs. M. E. Beasley

The Outside Trim and the Bracing under the Roof are Painted White and This, Together with the Comfortable Porch, Makes an Effective Appearance. There Are Five Rooms Nicely Finished in Paneling and Art Burlap

THESE bungalows show what a variety of pleasing designs can be evolved with a little ingenuity upon the part of the architect. The bungalow has many advantages on account of its convenience from the housekeeping standpoint; and this fact, combined with its extreme economy of construction, makes it very easy to understand the increasing popularity of this type of home.

Designed by John R. Ott

The Exterior Walls of This Attractive Little "Box" Bungalow Are Covered with Rough Boards and Battens. It Has Six Rooms and a Bath. Cost $1,000

Designed by William Mohr

This Compact Home Contains Five Rooms and a Bath. The Entrance Porch Is Made Prominent by the Gable Feature. Cost $800

Designed by Helen Lukens Gaut and O. C. Williams

The Climbing Roses and the Well-Placed Shrubbery Blend Exquisitely with the Exterior Finish of Pearl Grey and White

A Picturesque Bungalow

Contributed by Helen Lukens Gaut

THE spacious veranda, eight feet wide, of grey cement edged with red brick, extends across the front of the house, and beyond at one end for a distance of ten feet. The entire length is roofed with a pergola of heavy timbers, painted white and supported by round cement pillars with a circular topping of red brick. The interior is plastered, delicately tinted, and bedrooms, bath, hall, and kitchen are finished in white enamel. In the living room and the dining room the woodwork is in rich old ivory enamel, with the walls tinted a warm old gold. In the dining room the walls are covered with satin tapestry paper in forest design. Cost about $2,400.

Bungalow of Rustic Character

Contributed by Elva Elliott Sayford

SHOWN at the right is a bungalow of generous proportions which cost but $1,455 to build in California. The floor plan shows large rooms well placed, and the bedroom, separated as it is from the kitchen and living portion of the house by a small hall, is a most desirable feature. The exterior is of shingles, stained, and the pergola, covered with pretty flowering vines, adds greatly to the attractive appearance of the bungalow.

Designed by Alfred E. Gwynn

The Vine-Covered Pergola Is One of the Most Attractive Features of This House, and It Also Makes the House Look Much Wider

Two Effective Bungalows of Low Cost

Contributed by Mrs. E. C. Graham

A Bright and Cheerful Framework of Trees and Shrubs

IN BUILDING this bungalow the main idea was to get the greatest amount of comfort with the least expenditure of money. It cost about $900, and the plan is good in that it permits much elasticity as to cost. Outside, the house is weatherboarded, stained, and finished with white trim. Inside, the floors are of smoothly dressed pine and the woodwork is stained brown. One entire side of the kitchen is amply provided with cabinets, and all the plumbing fixtures are the best.

SCREEN PORCH
LAUNDRY TRAY
STORE-ROOM
KITCHEN 9'6"x11'6"
SINK
CUPBOARD
DINING-ROOM 11'6"x13'6"
BUFFET
SEAT
LIVING-ROOM 11'6"x24'6"
BEDROOM 10'0"x11'6"
CLOS.
BATH
BEDROOM 11'6"x11'6"
PORCH

Floor Plan

COMFORT is the most noticeable characteristic of this picturesque bungalow. It was built at a comparatively low cost, and the convenience of its interior arrangement makes it particularly interesting. The chimney is built of rough brick and the living room fireplace is finished in the same material. All the floors are double, the under floor being of spruce and the upper one of hard pine. The outside walls and roof are of the best quality of cedar shingles stained grey with white trim.

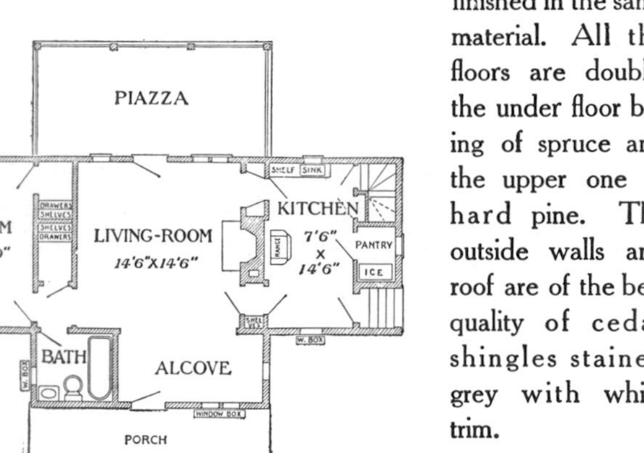

Floor Plan

An Inviting Exterior with Its Window Boxes and Trellis for Climbing Roses

Contributed by Mary H. Northend

Designed by C. W. Buchanan

A Very Unique Roof Effect with Exceptional Overhang in the Center to Shelter the Veranda

Designed by G. A. Howard

A Commodious Bungalow with a Fine Broad Porch. The Small Porch Set in the Roof Adds Much to the Attractiveness of This Design

Designed by C. W. Buchanan

The Extremely Broad and Rangy Gable Gives a Pleasing Effect

Designed by C. W. Buchanan

An Excellent Type of Dwelling of the Well-to-do Rancher. The Big Roomy Porch Is Especially Inviting

Four Charming Pasadena Bungalows

THESE excellent designs, while having considerable individuality, show very characteristic developments of this type of dwelling. The artistic setting of shrubbery is exceptionally fine, and is, of course, easily accomplished in California. The cost of these bungalows ranges from $4,000 to $6,000.

An Exceptionally Effective Design When Plenty of Ground Is Available. The Big Porch Is Ten Feet Wide and Extends Across the Entire Front and Around to Each Wing

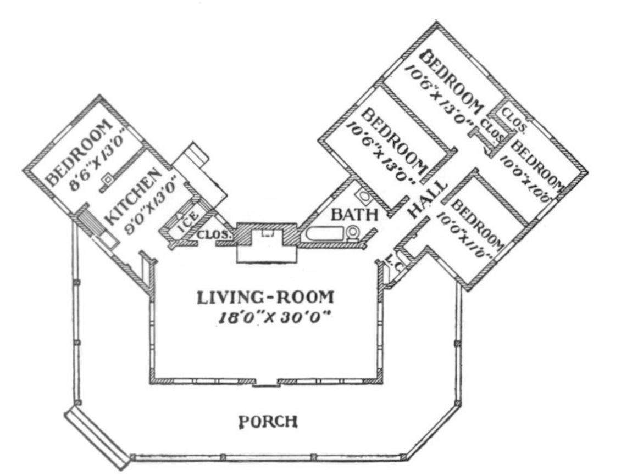

This Is a Most Unusual Plan. The Placing of the Wings Gives a Maximum of Light and Air

The Exposed Rough Timbering and Quaint Fireplace Give This Room an Old-Fashioned Charm

A Summer Bungalow of Distinct Merit

Contributed by Theodore M. Fisher and Victor S. Wise

THIS summer home is situated on the banks of a small river. The main object of this unique plan was to secure plenty of light and ventilation, especially in the living room. The corner of the porch next to the kitchen is improvised as a dining room in good weather. The family bedrooms are separated from the living room by an offset in which are placed a bathroom and linen closet. Cost $1,410.

Designed by
S. C. Guthrie

Designed by George Aspinwall

Inexpensive Bungalows

Contributed by Helen Lukens Gaut,
Pasadena, California

THESE six simple bungalows of the California type are very homelike and comfortable. They contain from three to five rooms. The same artistic setting of foliage can be used in a measure in any part of the country, although the growth is more luxuriant in California. These houses cost less than $1,000 to build, with the exception of the upper right-hand one which cost about $2,000.

Designed by
C. H. Anderson

Designed by J. F. Kavenaugh

The Cobblestones, Shingles, and Rustic Boards Make an Effective Exterior for This $2,000 Bungalow

SCREEN PORCH
CUPBOARD
KITCHEN 9'9" X 12'9"
BUFFET
DINING-ROOM 11'6" X 12'9"
CASES
LIVING-ROOM 18'6" X 16'9"
SEAT
PORCH
BEDROOM 11'0" X 11'6"
CLOS.
BATH
BEDROOM 11'0" X 11'6"
CLOS.
CLOS.
SEWING-ROOM 11'0" X 12'9"

Floor Plan

The Fireplace End of Living Room Makes a Cozy Corner

A Charming and Inexpensive Bungalow

Contributed by William Graham and Helen Lukens Gaut

THE cobblestone wall, pillars, and chimney are all capped with a layer of red brick which add a bit of rich color, blending effectively with the porch box filled with geraniums. The interior is rather "flat-like" in arrangement, but this is necessitated by the shape of the lot. The whole air of the bungalow is one of comfort and cheer.

Designed by H. D. Rounde

Six Attractive Bungalows

THE California bungalow has an exceptionally cozy, homelike atmosphere and is being used more and more in the East. The extreme overhang of the roof and the simple lines make these models very attractive. These houses cost from \$3,000 to \$4,000, except the center ones which cost between \$1,500 and \$2,500.

Designed by R. B. Young

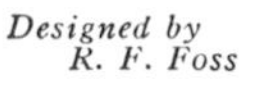

Designed by R. F. Foss

Designed by Greene & Greene

Picturesque Cottage at Marblehead, Massachusetts

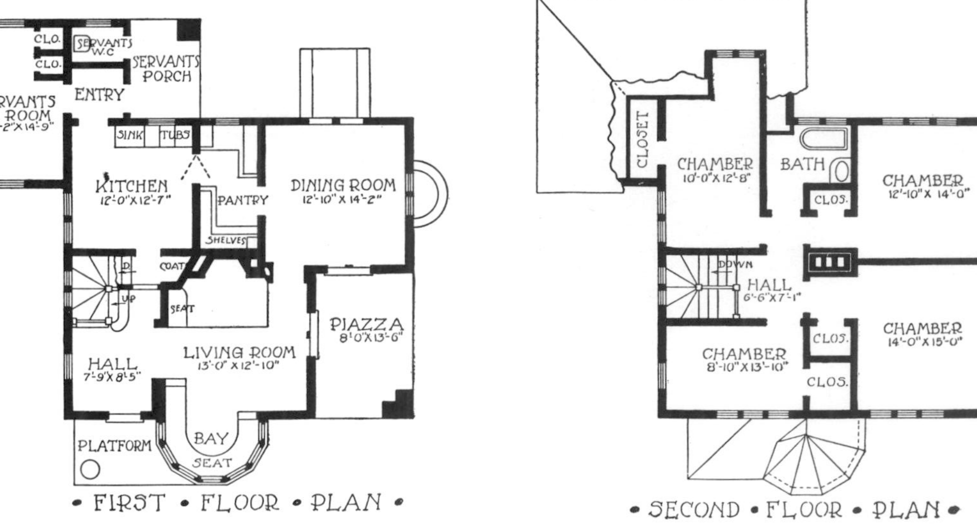

Floor Plans of Cottage at Left

Two Delightful Seashore Cottages

THE seashore claims some of our most charming homes. It seems as though the ocean inspires the architect to be simple and direct in his expression. The plaster house was designed by Thomas M. James of Boston, Massachusetts. The plans show excellent economy in arrangement, the privacy and homelike quality of all the different parts being well worked out. The casement windows with the small panes of glass, and the soft roof lines with the thatched roof effect, all help to give the exterior a quiet substantial air. The Tea House has an entirely different roof treatment. Its rustic pergola porch lends an inviting aspect to this house, with its shingles having the silver grey color of the rocks with which it is surrounded.

Tea House of Decidedly Rustic Character at Marblehead, Massachusetts

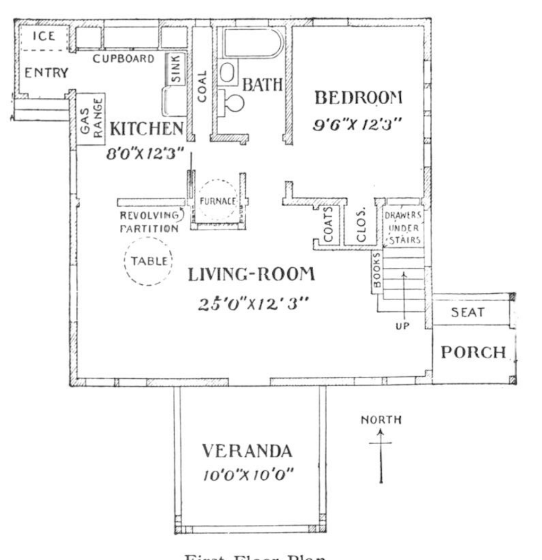

First Floor Plan

A Remarkably Compact House of Low Cost

View Showing Operation of the Pivoted Partition

An Easy Housekeeping Cottage

Contributed by Charles E. White, Jr.,
Chicago, Illinois

THIS comfortable house was designed and partly built by the owner. The plumbing and plastering were done by contract, but the balance of the work was accomplished by day labor. There is no cellar nor foundation wall, the sills being spiked to concrete piers, located six feet apart and rising to the sill level a foot above the ground. The frame work of 2-inch × 4-inch studding was erected on the sill and the frame was then boarded, furred, and lathed ready for the plasterers. The building was completed, ready for occupancy, in six weeks. An interesting feature of this house is the pivoted partition between the combination living room and dining room, and the kitchen. On the second floor is a large room with a balcony at one end and a sleeping porch at the other. Another feature particularly worthy of note is the large number of porches, there being three on the first floor and two on the second. This house cost the owner only $1,800, but if it had been constructed in the customary way it would have cost considerably more.

The China-Cabinet Side of the Partition

Designed by H. L. Wilson

This Charming Bungalow Has Seven Large Rooms. The Living Room and the Dining Room Are Paneled to the Plate-Rail and the Bedrooms Are Finished in White. Cost $2,500

Designed by B. G. Horton

Trailing Vines Add Much to This Cozy Little Home. It Has Four Rooms and a Bath on the First Floor and Two Rooms Above, All Well Planned. . Cost $2,250

Designed by Norman F. Marsh

There Are Four Rooms and a Bath in This Attractive Bungalow. The Square Lattice on the Two Bay-Windows and Door Provides a Simple Decoration

Designed by Sanford C. Wing

An Admirable Design for a Bungalow Built on a Hillside. It Has Five Rooms, Bath, Cellar, Screen Porch, Attic, and a Large Veranda, and It Cost Only $1,800

Four Picturesque Western Bungalows

THESE bungalows are extremely well designed and have a cozy and homelike atmosphere. They furnish a good example of what can be done with comparatively little money wisely spent.

Designed by R. B. Young

The Terraced Lawn and Cement Steps Add to the Effectiveness of This Bungalow

SCREEN PORCH
CLOSET
KITCHEN 9'6"X10'0"
DEN 9'6"X10'0"
BEDROOM 12'0"X14'0"
DINING-ROOM 14'0" X 20'0"
CHINA
CLOS.
BATH 8'0" X 10'0"
LIVING-ROOM 14'0" X 20'0"
BEDROOM 12'0"X15'0"
SEAT
CEMENT PORCH 6'9" X 23'0"

Floor Plan

Corner in the Living Room—a Cozy Ingle-Nook

A Simple Bungalow with Convenient Interior Arrangement

Contributed by Helen Lukens Gaut and W. H. Hill

THE broad expanse of roof with its wide overhang gives an excellent appearance to the exterior. As the porch is only partially covered, the lighting of the living room is unusually good. The interior woodwork is simple and always in good taste. The cost of this bungalow is $2,100, divided as follows: Masonry, $425; carpentry, $400; lumber, $275; millwork, $575; plumbing, $200; painting, $125; hardware, $50; electric wiring, $50.

Designed by W. H. Sawyer

Dark Brown Walls and White Trim Give This Little Home an Air of Individuality and Charm. It Has Five Rooms and a Bath and Cost about $2,000

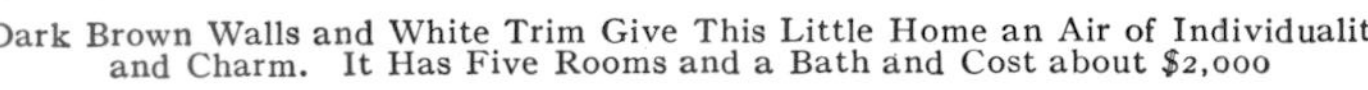

Designed by Edward C. Kent

The Gay Flowers and Pretty Lawn Give to This Bungalow a Most Attractive Setting. Inside There Are Seven Rooms and Bath, and It Cost but $2,500 to Build

A Comfortable Home Like This May Be Built for $2,000. Its Broad Eaves and Latticed Windows Are Quaint and Pretty. There Are Six Rooms

Designed by R. Mackey Frippe

The Craftsman Pergola and the Porch Rail Give This Six-Room Bungalow a Special Charm. The Living Room Has a Brick Fireplace. The Bungalow Cost $2,250

Four Attractive California Bungalows of Moderate Cost

THE interest of these distinctive little homes is due in part to their attractive design and is enhanced by the well-kept lawns and the surrounding foliage effects. The economy of this type of house is obvious when it is considered that none of those shown above cost over $2,500.

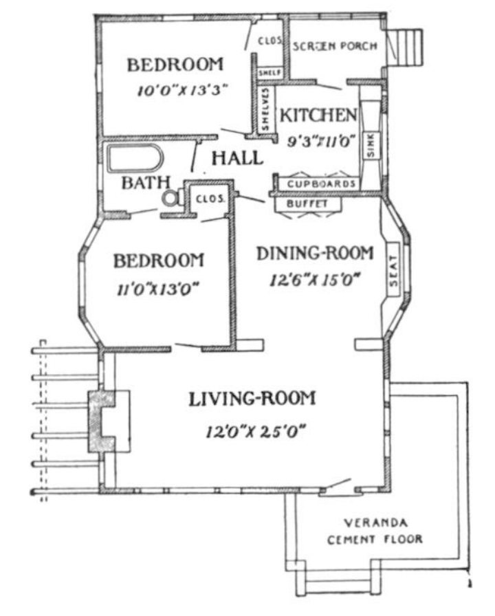

Floor Plan

Designed by W. G. Hanson

This House Owes Much of Its Character to the Attractively Placed White Trim. The Shrubs in the Foreground and the Trees in the Background Furnish a Very Picturesque Setting for the Bungalow.

TWO good features of this bungalow are the pretty front porch and the pergola on the side, the latter making a quiet rest-spot for afternoons. The exterior is of clapboards, stained and set off by the white trim which is admirably placed. In the interior the walls are plastered and tinted and the woodwork is of Oregon pine, stained. The house is modern and convenient, and was built for $1,800.

Two Attractive California Bungalows

Contributed by Helen Lukens Gaut

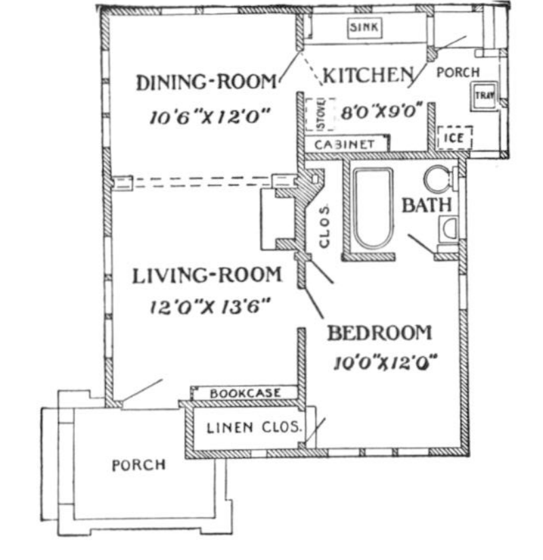

Floor Plan

The Overhanging Eaves and the Ornamental Gable Lend Interest to This House

THIS bungalow has four rooms, bath, and two comfortable porches. In California the house cost but $1,400. The combination of building materials, finish, and color scheme, shows cleverness and originality. For a small house the rooms are of good size. The living room has a color scheme of brown, green, and gold, and the bedroom is finished in rose pink and white.

The Rustic Effect of This Little Bungalow Blends Well with Its Environment

SLEEPING PORCH 10'0"x12'0"

BATHROOM

PASSAGE

PORCH

SINK

KITCHEN 12'0"x12'0"

STOVE

DINING-ROOM 12'0"x12'0"

LIVING-ROOM 16'0"x 24'0"

BOOKS SEAT BOOKS

PORCH

Floor Plan

The Living Room, Showing a Simple but Effective Interior

A Forest Home of Rustic Charm

Contributed by
Theodore M. Fisher and
Victor S. Wise

THE owners of this little cottage were the architects and they have shown good taste and careful planning in the arrangement. The living room is lighted on three sides, and with its fireplace and window seat makes a very cheerful room. The woodwork is stained a green brown and the spaces between the studding are covered with green burlap. The house cost about $1,400 without the bathroom plumbing.

Six Rooms and Bath Comprise This Tent-House Which Cost $650. The Walls Are Constructed of Clapboards and Duck

$500 Has Been Well Invested in This Little Tent-House of Five Rooms, the Interior Walls of Which Are Lined with Burlap

A Livable Feeling Pervades This House Which Cost but $300, and Which Has Three Rooms, Bath, and a Porch on Two Sides

Tent-Houses for Summer Days

Contributed by Helen Lukens Gaut, Pasadena, California

THE tent-house is primarily intended for summer occupancy, but can easily be adapted for all-the-year-round use in a warm climate. It may range from the ready-made tent that can be purchased and set on a wooden platform, to a house with up-to-date plumbing and conveniences.

This Attractive Tent-House of Four Rooms Would Make a Comfortable Summer Home for a Small Family. It Cost $350

This Is an Admirable Example of the Relation between House and Garden. The House Cost $800 and Has Four Rooms and Bath

Almost Hidden by Trees and Vines This Pretty Tent-House Bespeaks Coziness and Comfort, and Was Built for $300

Designed by A. S. Barnes

The Large Living Room and Broad Porch Are the Attractive Features of This Design

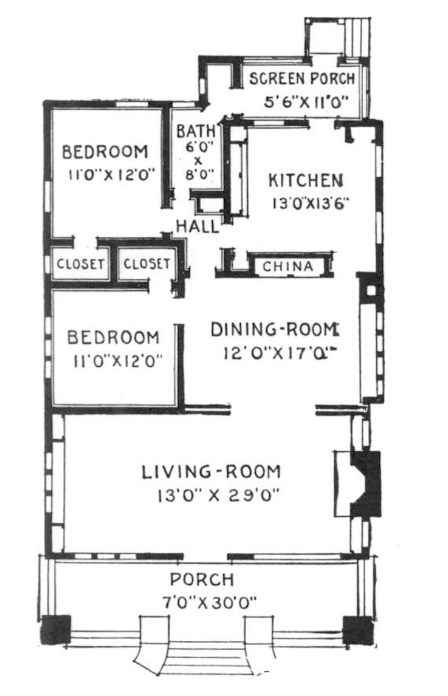

Floor Plan

View Showing Open Character of Living and Dining Rooms

An Artistic Bungalow of Moderate Cost

Contributed by
Helen Lukens Gaut and
W. H. Hill

THIS is a very substantial bungalow with a homelike atmosphere. The roof treatment is good and the cobblestone pillars and exposed chimney give an agreeable contrast to the clapboard walls, which are stained a dark brown. The cost was $1,900, divided as follows: Masonry, $250; carpentry, $325; lumber, $700; plastering, $140; plumbing, $225; painting, $160; electric wiring, $30; hardware, $50; tin and metal work, $20.

Designed by O. W. Sheldon

This Bungalow Is about as Simple as Can Be Built. It Contains Three Rooms. Cost Only $250

Designed by J. F. Manny

For a Small Fam ly This Five-Room Bungalow Offers Many Suggestions as to What May Be Accomplished in Home Building with Little Money. Cost $600

Small Attractive Homes of Low Cost

Designed by W. H. Winders

Cobblestones Form the Foundation of This Clapboard Bungalow. It Contains Six Rooms, Bath, and Screen Porch. All the Interior Walls are Plastered. Cost $1,500

Designed by H. M. Nickerson

This House Has Five Rooms, a Bath, and a Screen Sleeping-Room. The Cemented Terrace Porch Adds Greatly to Its Attractiveness. Cost $1,350

KITCHEN
9'0" X 13'0"

BATH

DINING-ROOM
15'0" X 18'0"

WORK-ROOM
8'0" X 15'0"

COAL

Basement Plan

Designed by Henry Troth

An $1100 Summer Cottage

Living Room—A Simple but Tasteful Interior

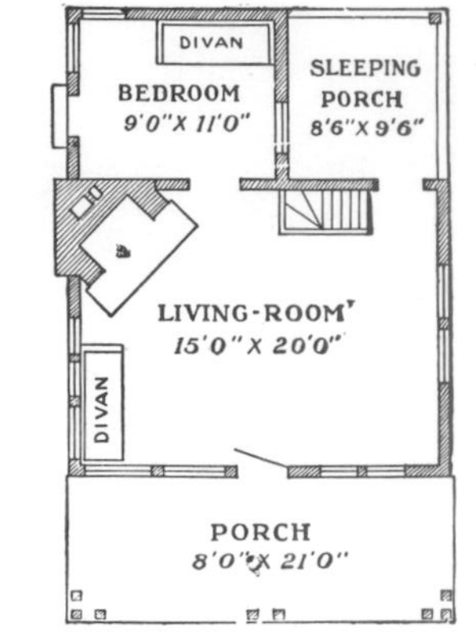

Ground Floor Plan

A STUCCO-COVERED summer cottage of simple design. On account of the slope of the lot, a very satisfactory basement floor has been obtained with little excavation and this makes the cottage more roomy than would be suspected at first glance. The setting of thick wood and the vine-covered porch make the picture very attractive.

The living room, which is wainscoted to a height of five feet, has an abundance of light, and the big fireplace adds much to the comfort of the room. A unique feature is the swinging stairway which leads to the upper rooms and which can be pushed up out of the way during the day or drawn up for safety at night.

Designed by A. D. Isbell

Designed by Alfred Heineman

Designed by G. M. Briggs and Wright & Callendar

California Bungalows

A GROUP of Pasadena houses of the bungalow type which has been so artistically developed in California. In several of these houses the graceful lines of the roof are accentuated by luxuriant vines and flowering plants. The exterior walls are either shingled or sided, the surface being left rough and stained thus making an inexpensive but effective finish. These models cost $1,000 to $3,000.

Designed by A. F. Miller

Designed by W. F. Hancock

Designed by Julius D. Lanning

Designed by Samuel Dailey

Front View of a Simple and Homelike Bungalow. The Pergola and French Windows Add Much to the Design

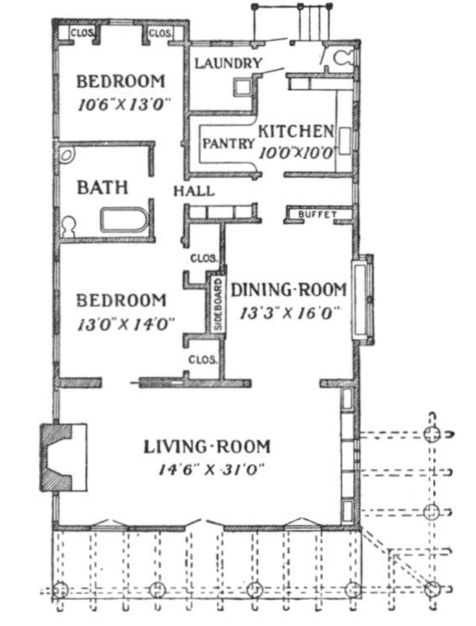

Floor Plan

The Dining Room Arrangement Is Effective

A Cozy Bungalow for $2,600

Contributed by William Graham and Helen Lukens Gaut

THE simplest of building materials—weather-boards — have been used, the architect depending upon the finishing touches to give that feeling of livableness without which no house is really a home. The attractive pergola with its substantial supports of rough plaster columns contributes largely to this feeling, with the hospitable French windows lending a charm all their own. Inside all of the rooms are so economically arranged that the problem of housekeeping in this bungalow would not be a difficult one.

An Ideal Warm-Weather Retreat

The Interior Is Suggestive of Sun and Air

Inexpensive Tent-House for the Summer Season

Contributed by Helen Lukens Gaut, Pasadena, California

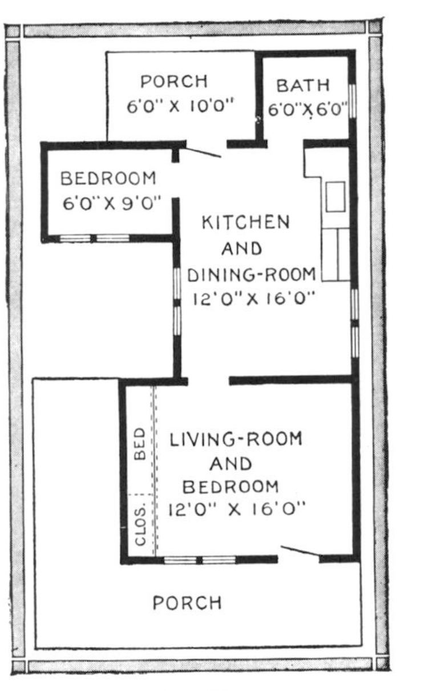

Floor Plan

A GOOD type of tent-house consists of a wooden floor set on foundation posts, a frame of 2×4 studding on which a base of clapboards is nailed with canvas above, and a roof of canvas or shingles, preferably shingles. If the roof is of canvas, a fly is necessary for use in summer, otherwise the heat would be oppressive. Canvas roofs are also objectionable because they are likely to leak in heavy rains. In the interior the partitions are usually of canvas or art burlap nailed on wooden frames. The tent-house shown here cost $300 to build, itemized as follows: Lumber, $100; plumbing, $100; labor, $75; canvas, $25.

The Porch Makes a Pleasant Outdoor Living Room

The Effect Is That of a Ship Putting Out to Sea

The Upper Rooms Are Reached by an Outside Stairway

A Cozy Corner in the Living Room

Boathouse and Camp in the Adirondacks

Henry Wilkinson, Architect

THIS ideal summer retreat is large enough to accommodate a forty-foot launch and several canoes below, with living room, two bedrooms, and bath on the second floor. The green of the roof, the grey of the walls and stone, and the white of the trim lend a delightful air of freshness to the building. The hall and living room woodwork is a grey brown with doors of solid brown ash without panels. The furniture is especially adapted in size and form to the rooms. The charm of the boathouse is largely due to the harmony and appropriateness of the woods, colors, and appurtenances chosen, and to the general air of refinement in evidence throughout.

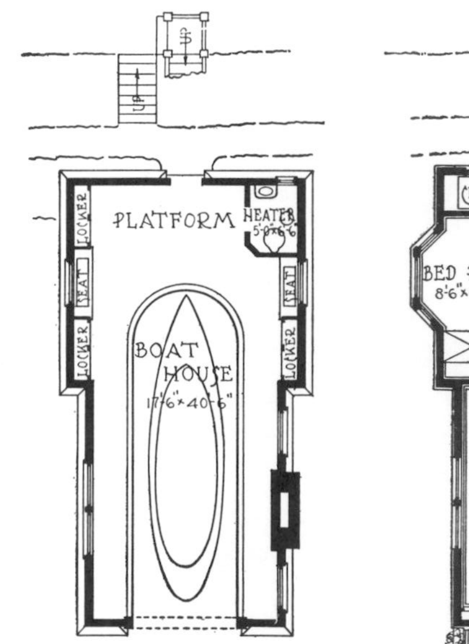

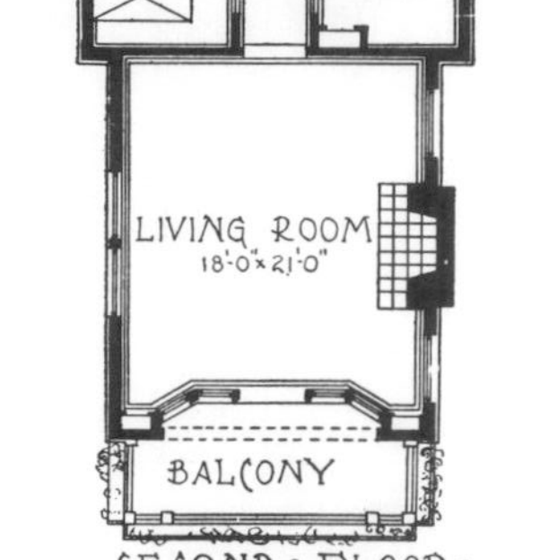

This Garage Was Designed to Harmonize with the Adjoining House. The Flower Boxes on the Doors Are a Unique Feature

Four Small House Garages

THESE garages while differing widely in appearance are all well designed, and can be built for very moderate cost. The attractive surroundings add much to the interest of these designs.

A Shingle Garage in a Most Attractive Setting of Trees and Vines

Plaster Garage with Sleeping Rooms on the Second Floor

A Well-Proportioned Concrete Garage of Substantial Appearance

Garage of Broad, Low Design with Shingled Exterior

Four Private Garages at Low Cost

THESE artistic designs are suggestive of the possibilities for the man who houses his own car. There is no more reason why the garage should be ugly than the residence itself, if a reasonable amount of study is devoted to its plan and construction.

An Interesting Feature of This Garage Is the Parapet Which Surrounds the Roof, Making an Admirable Place for the Children to Play Outdoors

A Small Garage of Shingles, Particularly Appropriate for the Country

This Simple Garage with the Exterior Walls of Pebble-Dash Is Well Adapted to a Small City or Suburban Yard

View of the House from the Northeast, Showing Screened Porch and Window Boxes

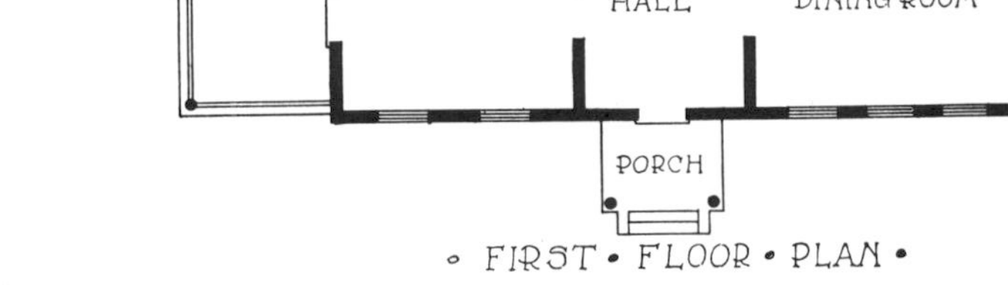

• FIRST • FLOOR • PLAN •

A Modern Colonial House

Richard E. Schmidt, Garden & Martin, Architects, Chicago, Illinois

THIS house has all the charm of the old colonial home combined with an air of modern life. The location of the trees and the arrangement of the terrace furnish a most attractive setting. The white walls, green blinds, and general effect recall the colonial building of the South, but the commodious living porch with its generous flower boxes proclaims the modern home. The plan is simple and yet affords all the luxuries that a twentieth century home is capable of, as evidenced, for instance, by the three bathrooms on the second floor, and the two on the third floor. The house was built in 1906 for Mr. C. D. Norton, Lake Forest, Illinois, at a cost of $12,000. For detail and interior views see plate following.

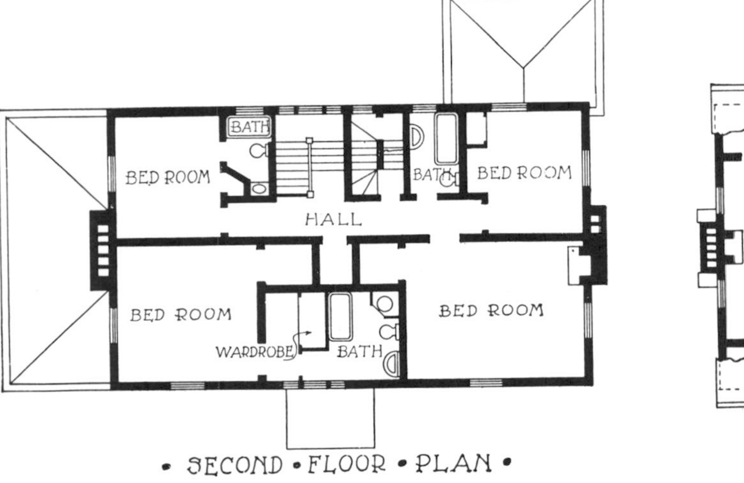

• SECOND • FLOOR • PLAN •

BATH
BED ROOM
BATH
BED ROOM
HALL
BED ROOM

• THIRD • FLOOR • PLAN •

The Staircase Hall and Living Room Beyond

The Fountain Seems to Echo the Delicacy of the General Design of the House

The Big Living Room, with Old Mahogany, Chintz-Covered Furniture, and New Wicker

A Modern Colonial House

Richard E. Schmidt, Garden & Martin, Architects, Chicago, Illinois

THE interior is full of quiet dignity. The lighting is particularly worthy of attention. There are no central fixtures to break the long, low appearance, lamps and side fixtures being used to give the necessary light and to add to the decorative effect. The walls and ceilings are kept in light tones, which combine well with the white woodwork and the simple dotted muslin curtains. For plans and exterior see plate preceding.

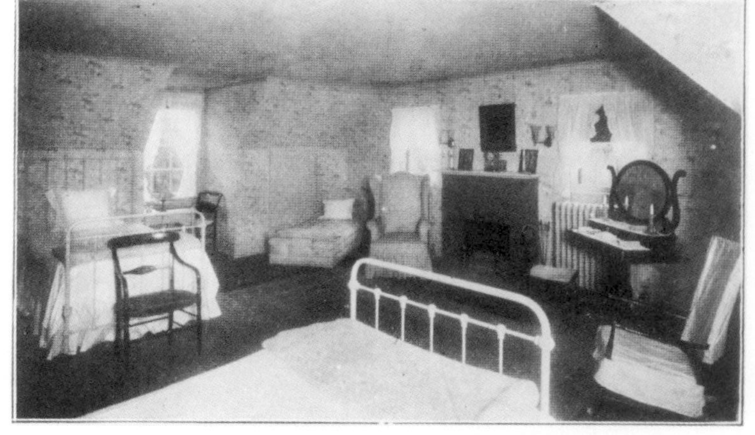

An Attractive Bedroom in the Third Story

South Front of Residence of Mr. A. H. Mulford, Oak Park, Illinois

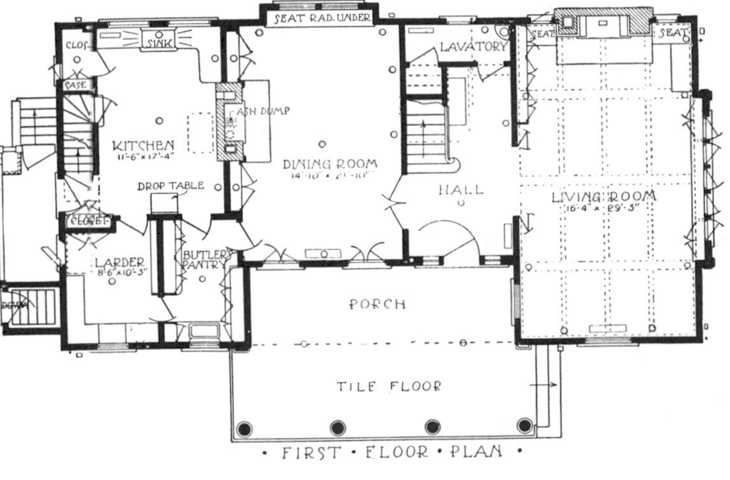

An Attractive Home with Shingled Exterior

A. G. Brown and James L. Fyfe, Associate Architects, Chicago, Illinois

A COUNTRY house like this with white trimmings always looks well in a setting of trees, shrubs, and flowers. The entire walls and roofs are covered with split cypress shingles. The base course is of hard-burned brick; the floor of the porch is of tile. The wood flower boxes add very little to the cost of a house, but lend much to its charm and domestic feeling. For rear view, elevations, and plans of second story and attic, see plate following.

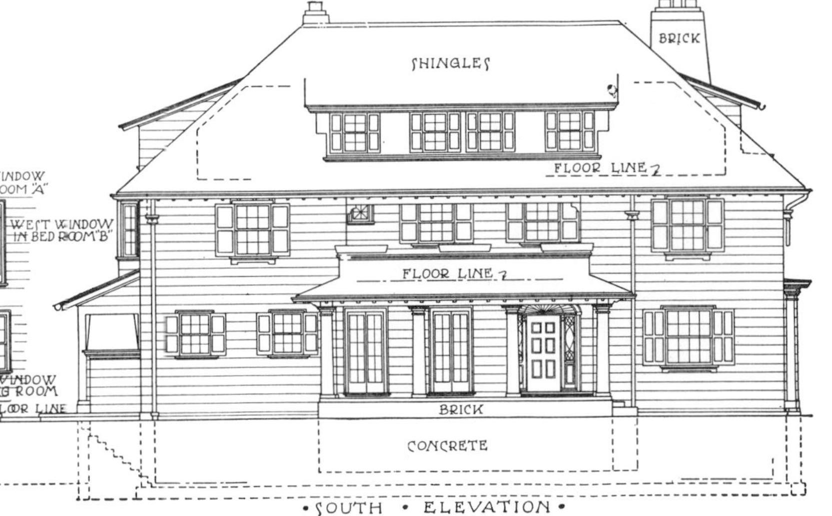

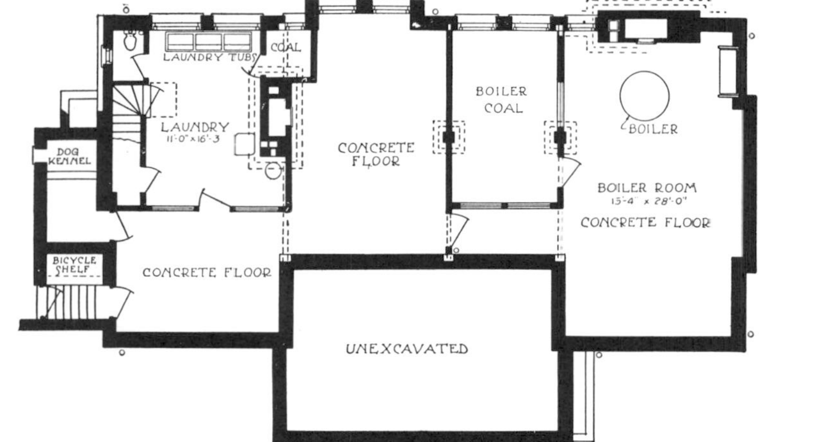

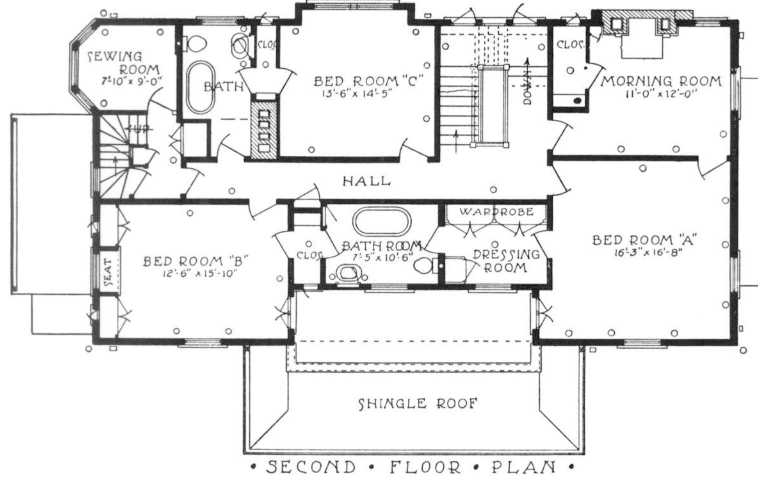

• SECOND • FLOOR • PLAN •

An Attractive Home With Shingled Exterior

A. G. Brown and James L. Fyfe, Associate Architects, Chicago, Illinois

THE rear of the house makes a very attractive appearance, showing how important it is that the back of a house receive as much study as the front. The big chimney gives dignity to the composition. The house was built in 1909. For front view, first story, and basement plan, see plate preceding.

Rear View of Mr. Mulford's Country House

• WEST • ELEVATION •

• EAST • ELEVATION •

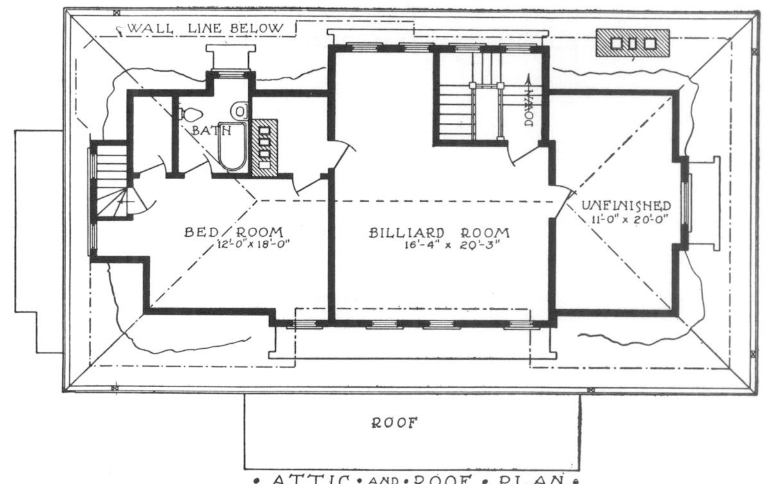

• ATTIC • AND • ROOF • PLAN •

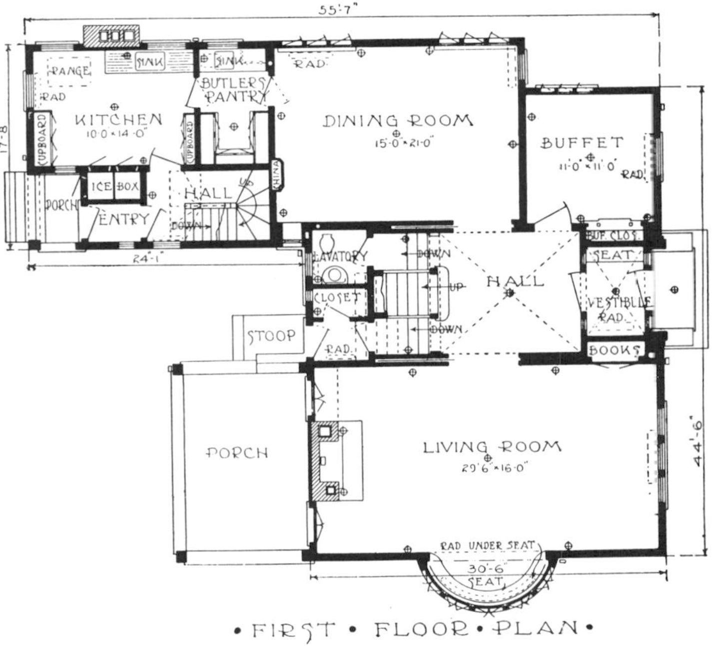

•FIRST • FLOOR•PLAN•

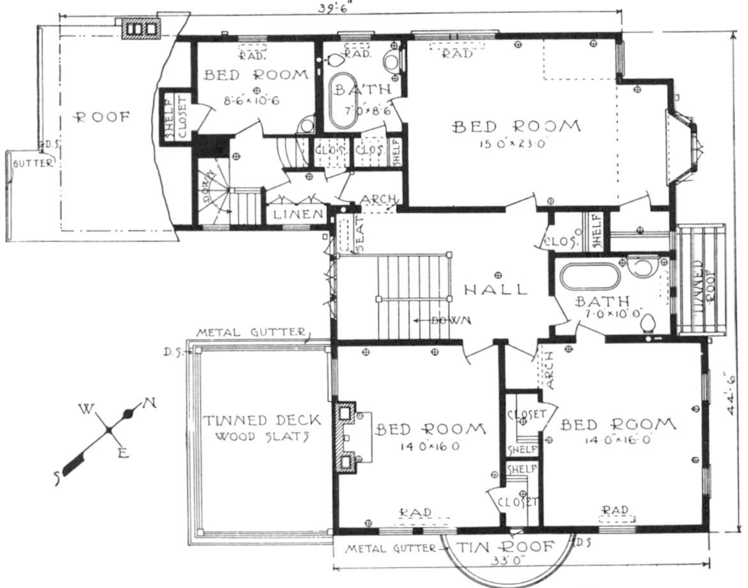

•SECOND • FLOOR • PLAN•

A Well-Designed Frame Dwelling Whose Chief Characteristic Is Simplicity

Arthur G. Brown, Architect, Chicago, Illinois

THIS frame house, which is the residence of Mr. Aylesworth, Wilmette, Illinois, has stucco outside on metal lath, with half timber treatment in the second story. The overhanging bays lend interest and give character to the simple lines of the house. The roof is covered with shingles dipped in stain. The living and dining rooms have birch mahogany finish, the balance of the main portion has white wood with white enamel finish, and mahogany doors. The kitchen portion is finished in Georgia pine, stained. The house was built in 1905 and cost $14,000.

• WEST • ELEVATION •

A Colonial Plaster House

A. Raymond Ellis, Architect, Hartford, Connecticut

THIS house illustrates the substantial character that can be given a frame house covered with stucco. The red shingle roof harmonizes well with the grey plaster, the brick chimney, and green blinds. The building faces west. The interior finish consists of mahogany in the dining room, oak in the den, and white wood in the living room, hall, and on the second floor. There are hardwood floors in the main rooms. The house is heated by hot water. It was built, in 1910, in Hartford, Connecticut, for Mr. W. C. Walker, at a cost of approximately $15,000.

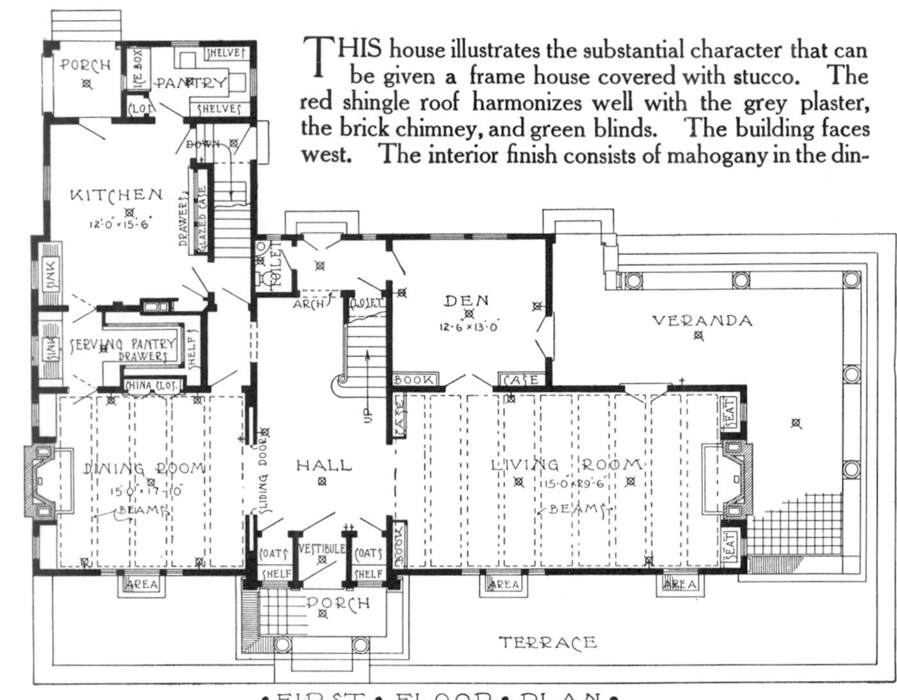

• FIRST • FLOOR • PLAN •

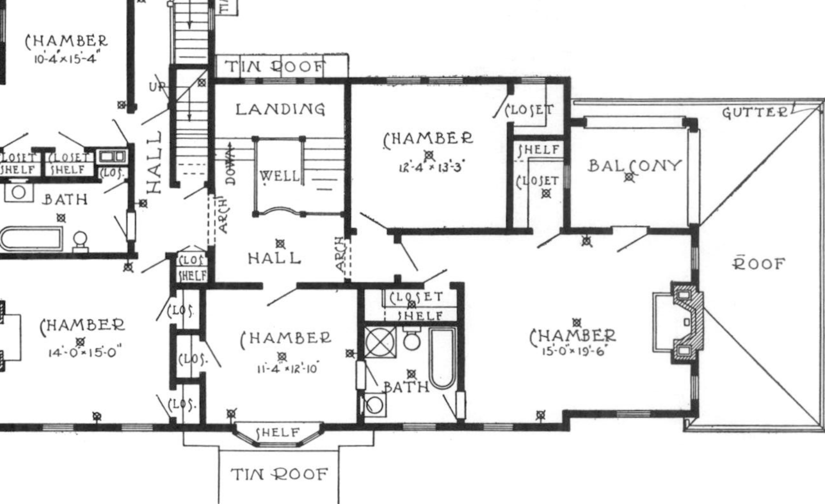

• SECOND • FLOOR • PLAN •

Residence of E. D. Moeng on the Shore of Lake Michigan, Chicago, Illinois

A Tasteful Living Room with Soft Lighting Effects

Hallway and Stairs

A Lake Shore Residence of Novel Exterior

Lawrence Buck, Architect, Chicago, Illinois

THE local material—pebbles from the beach—has been used effectively on the exterior. The roof is of a gray-green tile, and the trim is stained brown to match the color of the branches of the trees. The staircase window has a leaded glass design of a rose tree in soft tones of green and rose white. Other windows have designs of leaded stained glass suggesting the stories of Knighthood. The fireplace and the circular window of the living room are treated in an unusual way, the fireplace having a copper hood finished verde antique, inset with a panel of glass mosaic. For plans and entrance detail, see plate following.

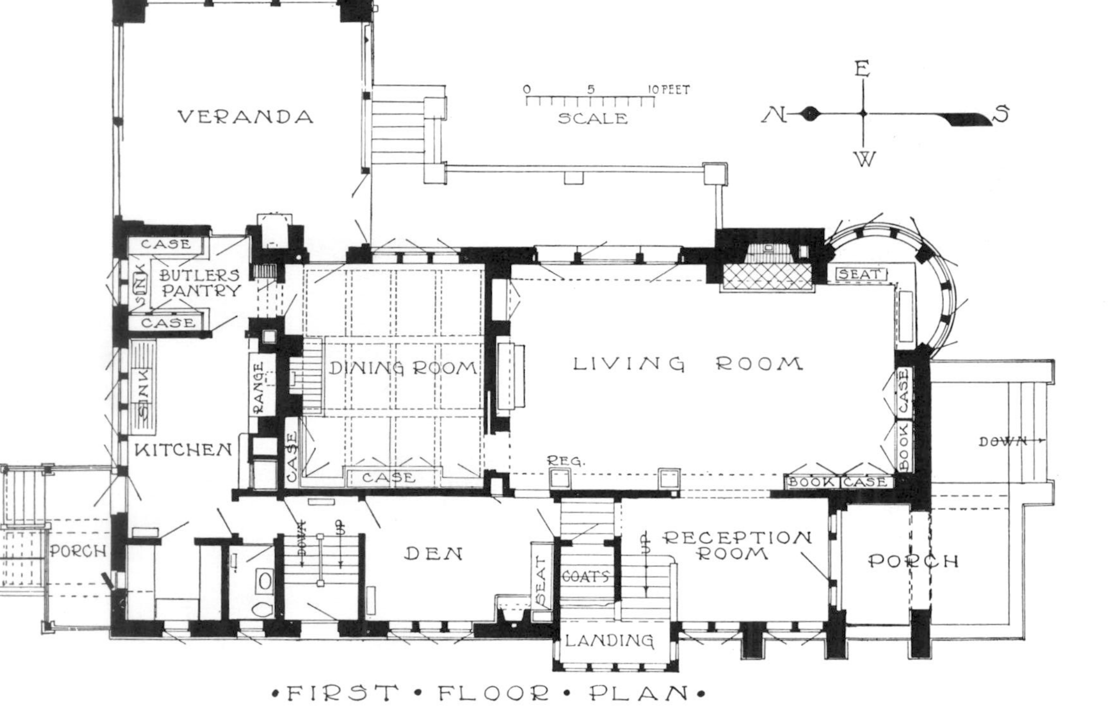

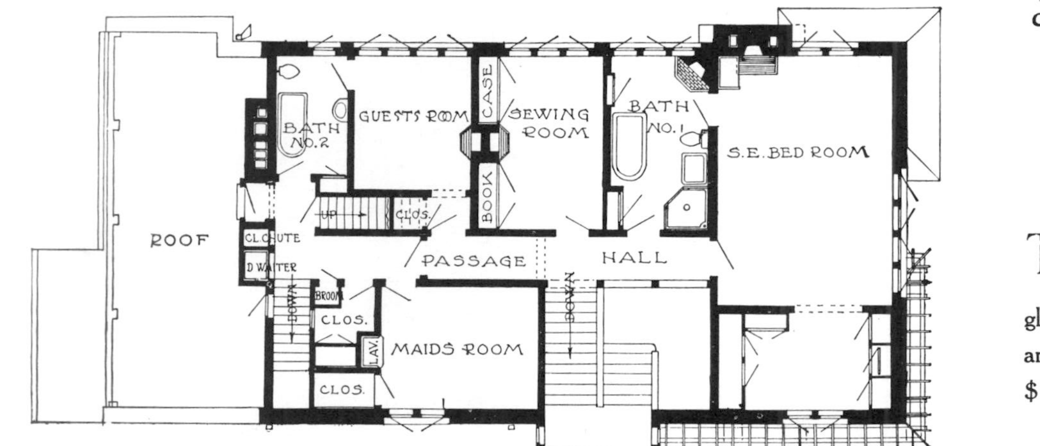

A Lake Shore Residence of Novel Exterior

Lawrence Buck,
Architect,
Chicago, Illinois

THE house is so planned that all the principal rooms have the advantage of the lake view. The veranda makes a delightful out-of-doors room with its small fireplace, screens, and glazed sash, the latter dropping into pockets in the wall. The woodwork of the living room and hall is of birch, stained a gray brown. The house was built in 1909 at a cost of $14,000. For exterior and interiors, see plate preceding.

A Well-Built Brick and Plaster House

A. Raymond Ellis, Architect,
Hartford, Connecticut

THE combination of plaster with brick in the lower story very often gives a lighter effect to a house. On the other hand, the use of brick in the lower story, in preference to carrying the plaster to the ground, does away with the danger of having the plaster when near to the ground disintegrate on account of being exposed almost constantly to the moisture of the ground and the bushes. A red brick has been used with a green slate roof. The house faces west. The interior has hardwood finish and floors, tile bathrooms, and hot-water heat. It is located in Hartford, Connecticut, and was built in 1910 for Mr. C. E. Walker at a cost of approximately $17,000.

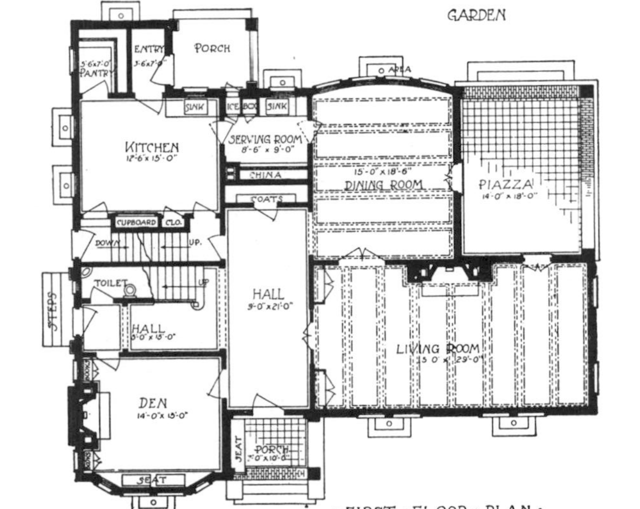

• FIRST • FLOOR • PLAN •

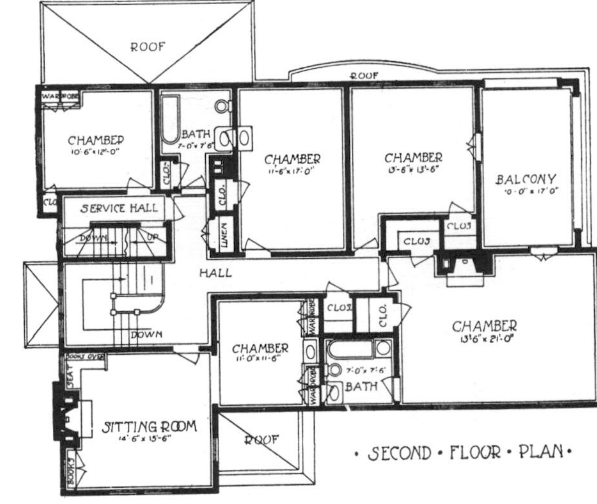

• SECOND • FLOOR • PLAN •

A Fine Propotiron and Balance in the Design Very Materially Helped by the Heavy Growth of Vines. The Living Porch Is at the East End and the Terrace Pergola at the West

Looking into the Dining Room from the Living Room

From the HOUSE BEAUTIFUL MAGAZINE

A Thatched House

Albro & Lindeberg, Architects

THOSE who have traveled in England remember the homelike aspect of the straw thatched house. This house is one of the examples in this country where the architects have used the shingles to produce a similar effect which in this case is very successful. The house is of frame covered with stucco over wire lath. The yellow sand of the vicinity gives the stucco a warm buff color. The blinds are a pale green, all other exterior woodwork is unstained and allowed to weather. It is the summer home of Mr. Edward T. Cockroft at Easthampton, Long Island.

• FIRST • FLOOR • PLAN •

A Frame and Plaster Suburban Home

George W. Maher, Architect, Chicago, Illinois

THIS attractive dwelling with its magnificent setting of foliage is the home of Mr. Frederick Sutton, Kenilworth, Illinois. It is a frame house with expanded metal covered with a fine texture of rough cast cement plaster and shingled roof. The interior of the house is well worth study. On entering, the whole house opens up before you, the staircase and dining room being thrown directly into the large finely proportioned living room. The interior trim of the living and dining rooms is fumed oak, and the bedrooms are finished in enamel white. The motif of the lotus flower conventionalized runs through the design of the details. The house was built in 1908 at a cost of 25 cents per cubic foot.

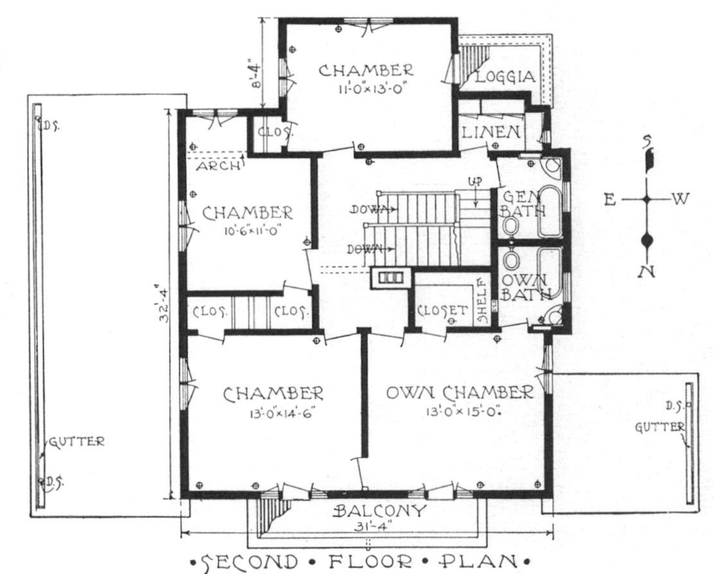

• SECOND • FLOOR • PLAN •

A House of Stucco with Gable-Roof Treatment, Kankakee, Illinois

This Library Shows the Effect of Harmonious and Artistic Treatment of Interior Decoration

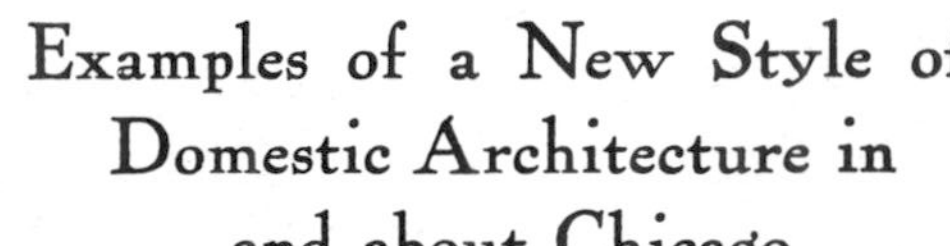

Examples of a New Style of Domestic Architecture in and about Chicago

Frank Lloyd Wright, Architect, Chicago, Illinois

THE chief characteristics of this style are the harmonious relation of the interiors and exteriors and the broad and simple treatment devoid of unnecessary ornamentation, relying upon the proportions, color, and arrangement to obtain a pleasing effect.

Corner in Living Room of a Home in River Forest, Illinois, Showing Artistic Grouping about the Fireplace

This House Shows a Hip Roof Treatment with the Very Flat Pitch Characteristic of This Style. The Exterior Walls Are Principally of Wood. Located at Evanston, Illinois

North Front Showing Drive and Porte Cochere

View of Terrace from Lake

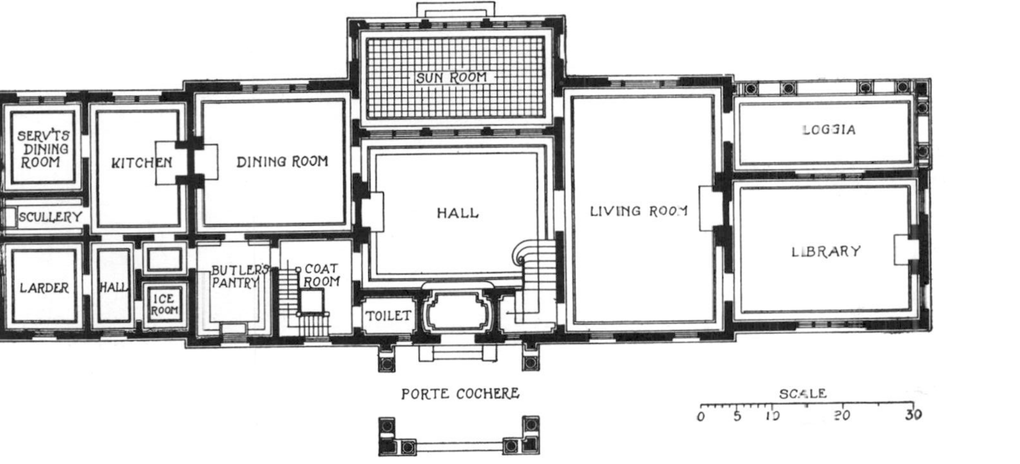

View of Library Loggia from Terrace

A Fireproof Country Mansion of Distinct Colonial Character

James Purdon, Architect, Boston, Massachusetts

THIS residence of Charles L. Harding, Esq., Dedham, Massachusetts, has the exterior walls faced with "tapestry" brick in deep shades; the columns and trimmings are of buff Indiana limestone; and the roof is covered with moss green dull-glaze tile in flat shingle shapes. The house is so planned as to have practically every living room and bedroom exposed to the south, the staircases, etc., being arranged on the north side. The building is entirely fireproof, the outside walls being of brick furred on inside with hollow terra cotta blocks and plastered direct thereon; all floors, partitions, stairs, ceilings, etc., are constructed of terra cotta and steel and reinforced concrete. The house was built in 1910 and cost, complete, 63 cents per cubic foot. For interiors see plate following.

SERV'TS DINING ROOM · KITCHEN · DINING ROOM · SUN ROOM · HALL · LIVING ROOM · LOGGIA · LIBRARY · SCULLERY · LARDER · HALL · ICE ROOM · BUTLER'S PANTRY · COAT ROOM · TOILET · PORTE COCHERE

SCALE 0 5 10 20 30

FIRST FLOOR PLAN

BALCONY · DAY NURSERY · BOY'S ROOM · BATH · CHAMBER · BATH · CHAMBER · BOUDOIR · LOGGIA · NIGHT NURSERY · BATH · MAID'S ROOM · STAIR HALL · LINEN · BATH · CLOSET · CHAMBER · BALCONY

SECOND FLOOR PLAN

Library Showing Door on Left Leading out upon Loggia

Sun Room Looking Toward Terrace and Lake

Dining Room Showing Fireplace with Facing of Black and Gold Egyptian Marble

Entrance Hall Looking Toward Dining Room. Front Door and Stairs on Left

A Fireproof Country Mansion

James Purdon, Architect,
Boston, Massachusetts

Library: Walls and ceilings of weathered English oak; floors of dull blue unglazed Grueby tile; mantel carved white Indiana limestone.

Sun Room. Walls of "tapestry" brick: floors of moss green dull-glaze Grueby tile; doors of mahogany with leaded plate glass; fountain of Italian Carara marble.

Dining Room: Walls and finish including mantle of carved dark Tabasco mahogany; mahogany furniture; blue leather panels in walls and seat coverings; ceiling with ornamental plaster beams; crystal electroliers.

Entrance Hall: Walls of French Caen stone; doors Tabasco Mahogany; fireplace facing of "tapestry" brick in deep tones, stairs, Caen stone finish; balustrade, wrought bronze finish with mahogany hand-rail. For plans and exterior views, see plate preceding.

Brick and Plaster Residence of Mr. J. Fletcher Skinner, Oak Park, Illinois

Interior of Veranda Which Is Finished in Oak with Cement Floor

A Well-Designed Suburban Mansion

Charles E. White, Jr., Architect, Chicago, Illinois

THE exterior is treated with an interesting combination of brick and plaster work, the cement plaster being applied directly to waterproofed common brick. Roofs are covered with slate. The interior design is carried out in simple elegance. The house was built in 1908 at a cost of $38,000. For views of interior see plate following.

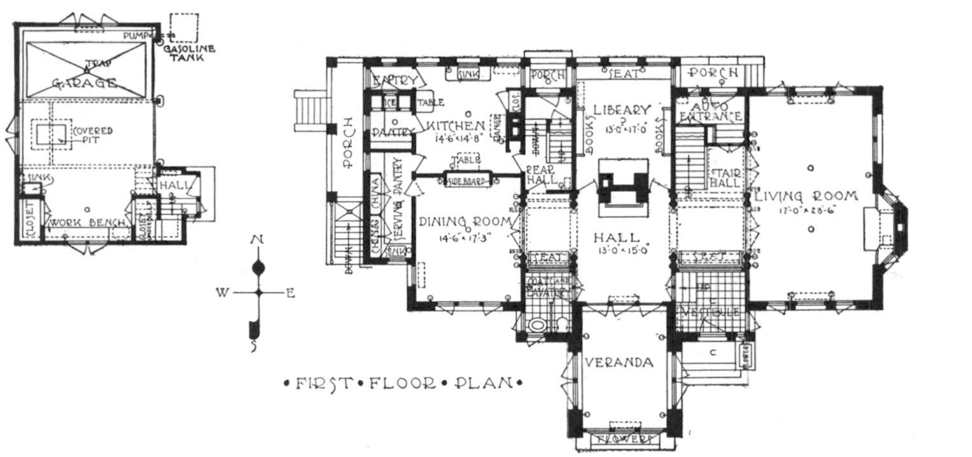

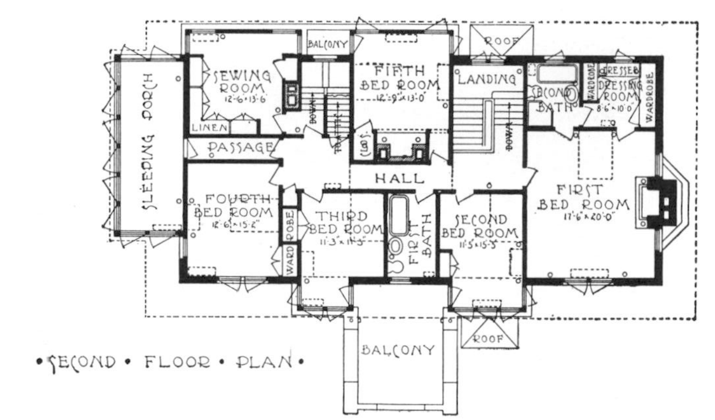

PLATE 93

Hall Fireplace with View of Double Library Entrance and Staircase

A Comfortable Looking Corner in the Living Room

Looking from Living Room down the Hall towards Dining Room

View of Dining Room Showing Oak Paneling

A Well-Designed Suburban Mansion, *Charles E. White, Jr., Architect, Chicago, Illinois*

These interiors of Mr. Skinner's residence show the delightful openness and charming design of the living rooms. For plans and exterior, see plate preceding.

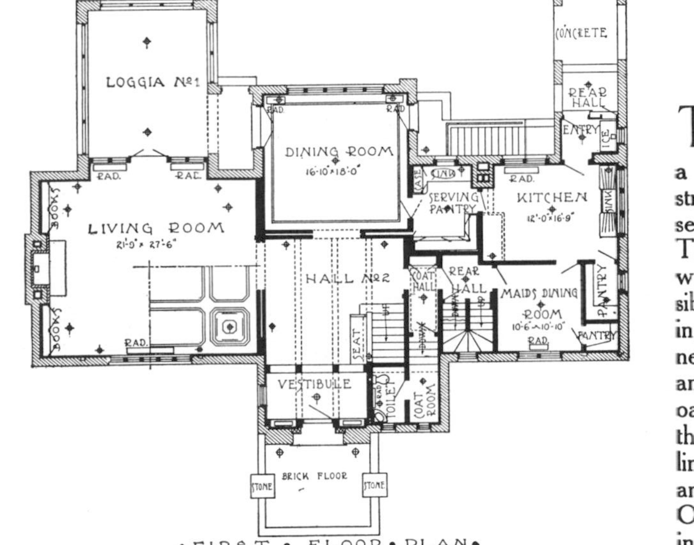

•FIRST • FLOOR • PLAN•

A Substantial Brick Mansion

Spencer & Powers, Architects, Chicago, Illinois

THE plan of this house has been carefully worked out and embodies all modern improvements. The house is built on a corner lot, the kitchen and the garage portion facing one street, and built up to the lot line. The entrance faces east and sets back a ways from the road to give a chance for the terracing. The living porch has been located on the garden side with south, west, and north exposure, and has been placed so that it is accessible from the living room and from the dining room. An interesting feature of the plan is the fact that the garage has been connected with the house. The interior has been treated in a simple and dignified manner. The living rooms and halls are trimmed in oak, and the bedrooms in birch stained, with oak floors in all of these rooms. The service portion has birch trim painted, with linoleum on the floors. The floors of the loggia, front entrance, and terrace are of brick laid in concrete. The house is situated in Oak Park, Illinois, and was completed for Mr. E. W. McCready in June, 1908. For exterior details see plate following.

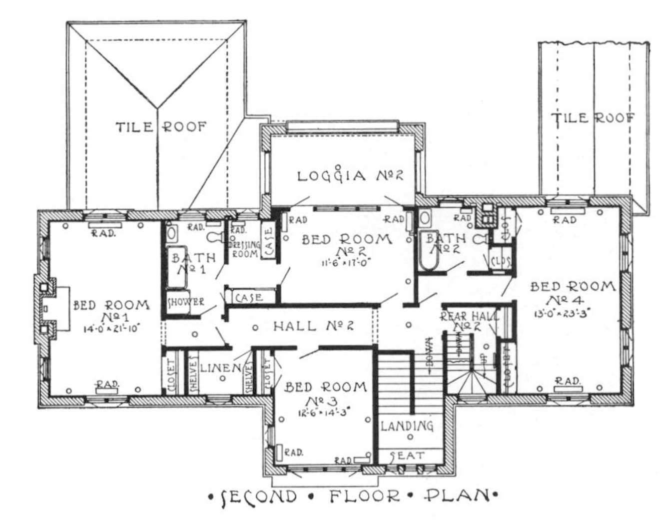

•SECOND • FLOOR • PLAN•

A Substantial Brick Mansion

Spencer & Powers, Architects, Chicago, Illinois

BRICK is a favorite material for the more costly city and suburban homes, not only on account of the fire-resisting qualities of the material, but also on account of the variety of beautiful textures and color effects that can be obtained in a well-laid brick wall. In this exterior a medium tan-colored Norman brick has been used with the horizontal joints raked out and the vertical joints made flush, thus accentuating the horizontal lines of the design. The roof is of Cloverport, Kentucky, red shingle tile. The entrance faces east. Casement windows with a simple but rich leaded glass design have been used throughout, except in the kitchen portion, where the usual double hung window has been installed. For plans and exterior showing garage see plate preceding.

Front Entrance of Dwelling with Garage in the Background

Dining Room with Entrance to Library at the Left

An Attractive Country Residence Combining Elegance With Good Taste

Henry K. Holsman, Architect, Chicago, Illinois

THIS large and well-designed house is the residence of Mr. George Webb, Oak Park, Illinois, and is an excellent illustration of the beauty of preserving simple lines even in costly houses. The exterior walls are entirely of brick, the facing being a rough brick of varying shades. The second story is plastered with stucco to lighten the appearance. The roofs are covered with clay tile. The exterior porch and floors are reinforced concrete for the porches, and tile and brick for the terraces and finished floors. The interior construction is of wood with steel columns and girders, cement plaster walls, and hardwood trim and floors throughout. The landscape work was laid out by the architect and completed by the nurseryman. The house was completed in 1910, and cost about 22 cents a cubic foot.

Living Porch and Balcony Alcove on Side Towards the River

Main View of House Showing the Broad Expanse of Lawn, the Pergola at the Left, and the River Beyond

A Modern Half-Timber House

Harvey Wright, Architect, Chicago, Illinois

THE lower story is entirely of plaster while in the second story the half-timber treatment is used for decorative purposes, the smaller plaster surfaces making a pleasing contrast to the broad areas and arch treatment below. A strong line of demarkation between the two stories is obtained by having the second project beyond the first. The house is the residence of Mr. A. J. Farley, Wheaton, Illinois.

Living Room Showing the Brick Fireplace and Staircase Platform

Bedroom Having Decided Colonial Feeling with Its White Woodwork and Mahogany Furniture

Apartment Building of Excellent Design

Spencer & Powers, Architects, Chicago, Illinois

THIS building, which contains eighteen apartments, is located on Garfield Boulevard, Chicago, Illinois, and was built in 1911 at a cost of about $45,000. The exterior is a dark red shade of paving brick. The interior trim is of oak in the halls, living rooms, and dining rooms, and of birch in the bedrooms, kitchens, and bathrooms. The six three-room flats at the west end of the building have built-in folding beds, thus affording practically the same accommodations as the other flats in the building which have four rooms. The flats rent for $37.50 to $50 per month.

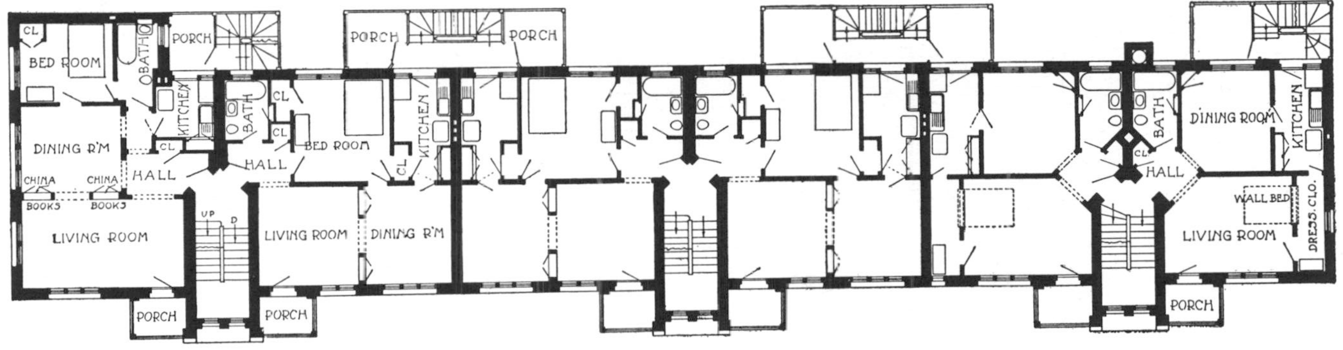

LAUNDRY
FRUIT CLOSET
FRUIT CLOSET
OPEN BASEMENT
LOT LINE
TO SEWER
LOT LINE

• BASEMENT • PLAN •

Suburban Flat Building

E. E. Roberts, Architect, Chicago, Illinois

THIS building being outside of the city limits is constructed of frame with stucco finish on the exterior and painted wood trim. The advantage of this type of building is that it can be made to look like a private residence by having a pitched roof, while there is enough space around it to permit of trees and shrubs. Built in 1910 at Oak Park, Illinois, for Mr. B. P. Horton. The cost of the building was approximately $11,000 and both apartments rent for $62.50 per month.

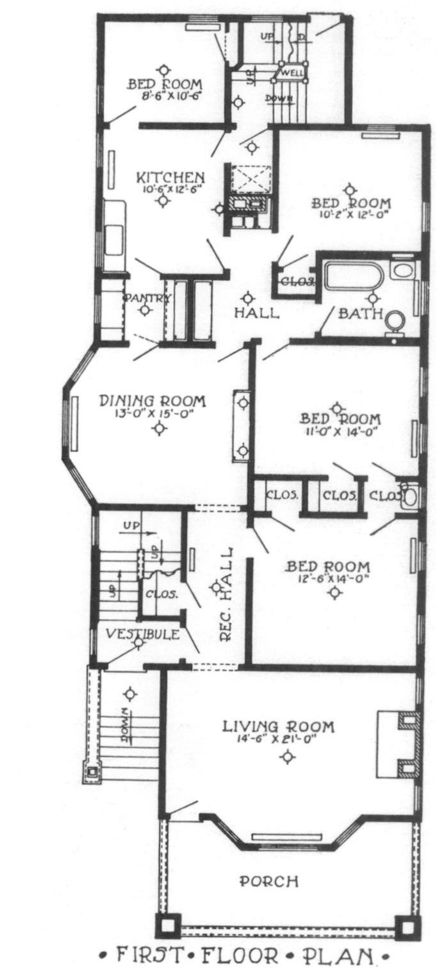

• FIRST • FLOOR • PLAN •

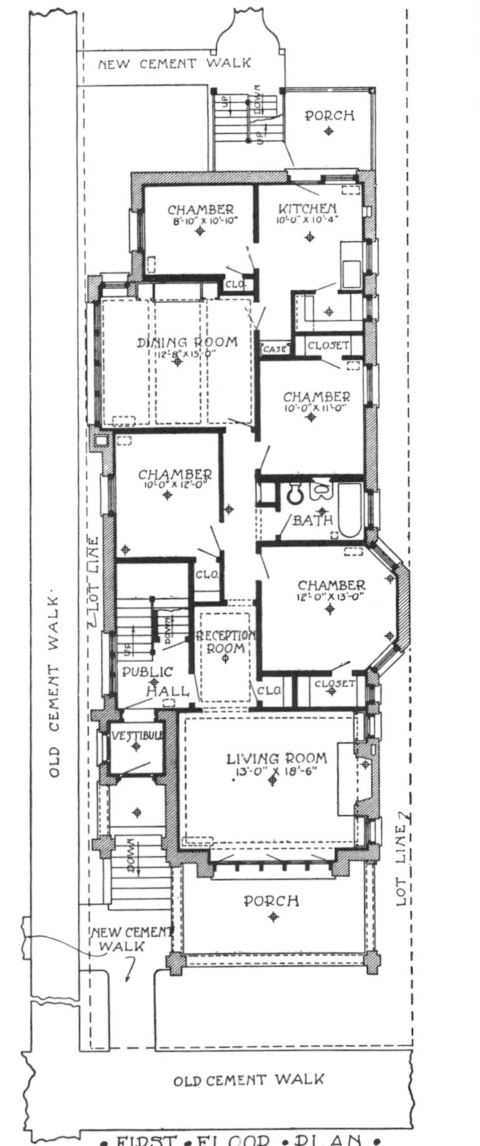

Courtesy of the NATIONAL BUILDER, Chicago, Illinois

Two-Family Apartment Building in a Large City

Perry & Thomas, Architects, Chicago, Illinois

THE exterior is of pressed brick with Bedford stone trim, which forms a pleasing combination with an atmosphere of solidity due to the absence of projecting metal or wood cornices. Access to the second-floor apartment is provided by an open stairway in the public hall, from which the door to the first apartment opens. There is a porch on each floor entirely separate from the entrance porch. The building is finished in hardwood throughout, and is heated by hot water. The living rooms have brick mantels and built-in bookcases. The dining rooms have sideboards, and the closet room is ample. The total estimate of cost is $10,498.78, of which some of the principal items are as follows: Excavating and masonry, $3,266.08; lumber, $1,166.42; mill work, $1,198.85; carpenter labor, $983.79; plastering, $394.20; plumbing, $600; heating, $1,200. The estimated cubic feet of building from bottom of cellar to roof, not figuring the rear porch, is 60,588, which makes the cost of this building about 17 cents per cubic foot.

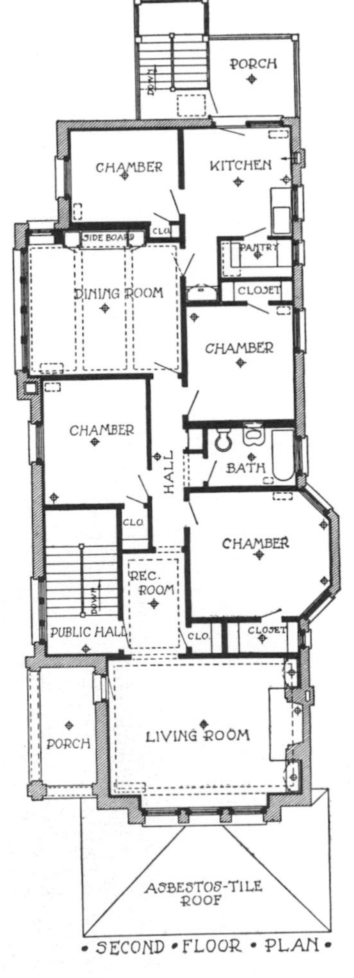

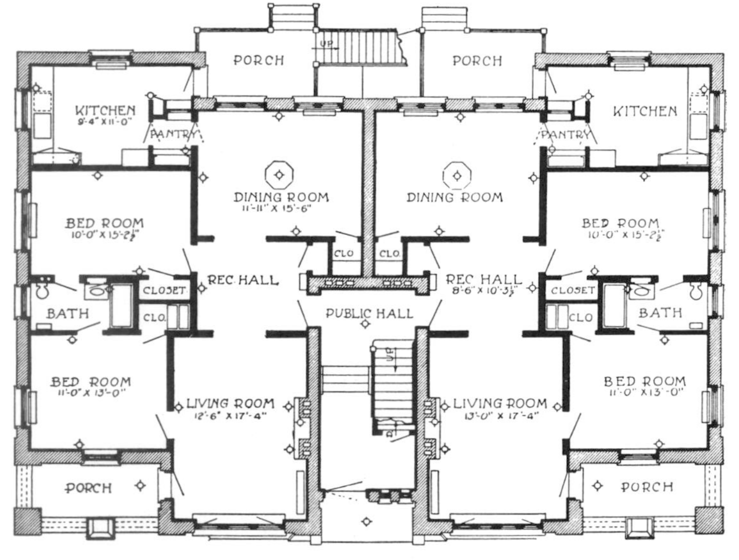

• FIRST • FLOOR • PLAN •

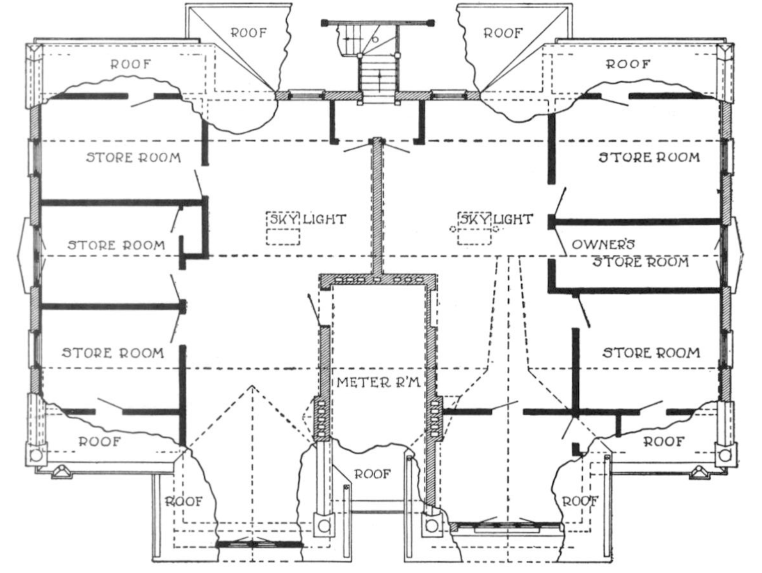

• ATTIC • FLOOR • PLAN •

A Pleasing Group of Apartments

E. E. Roberts, Architect, Chicago, Illinois

IN this building a successful attempt has been made to get away from the box-like appearance of the ordinary flat building by an interesting treatment of openings and pitched roofs, and the introduction of gables. The attic space thus supplied permits the location of the storerooms upstairs instead of in the basement, as is the usual custom. The half-timber motif in the gables adds a great deal of life to the composition. These apartment buildings, of which there are three, were erected at Oak Park, Illinois, in 1907, for Mr. Luther Conant at a cost of about $19,000 per building. The apartments rent for $50 per month.

Living Room Looking Toward Entrance Hall

Dining Room with South Exposure

A Modern City Apartment Building

William H. Pruyn, Jr., & Company, Architects, Chicago, Illinois

THE exterior is of red paving brick with stone trimmings. A nice feature is the fact of there being two porches, one off the living room and one off the dining room. The back staircase is arranged so that it does not protrude beyond the rear wall of the building. All the rooms are on the outside, thus securing a maximum of light and air. The living room and reception hall are trimmed in birch mahogany, the dining room in light weathered oak, the bedroom in white enamel, and the kitchen in natural oak. The front porches have reinforced concrete floors and Spanish green tile roofs. The building was erected in 1912 at a total cost of $19,000. The apartments rent for $42.50 to $50.

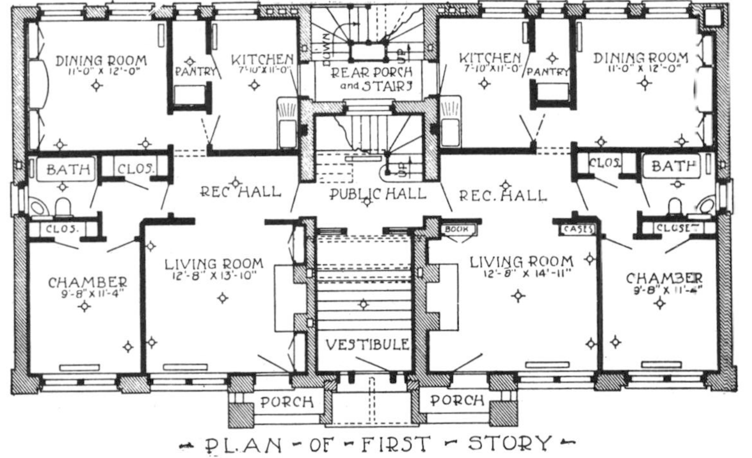

– PLAN – OF – FIRST – STORY –

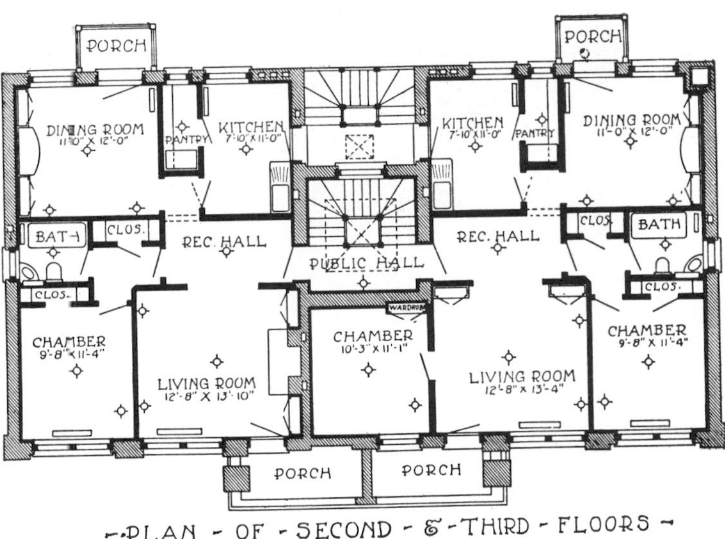

– PLAN – OF – SECOND – & – THIRD – FLOORS –

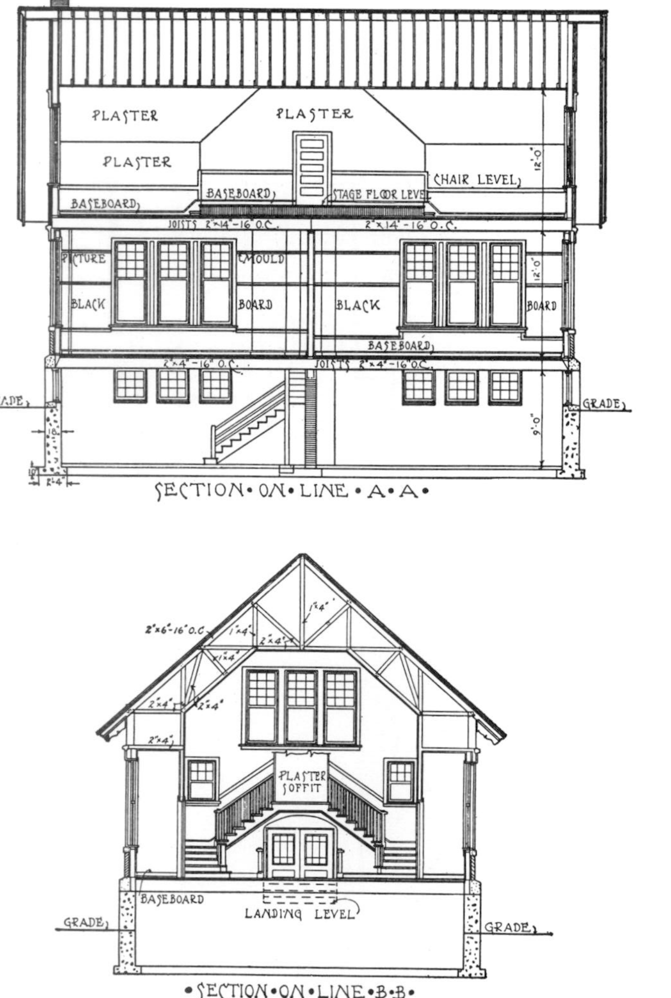

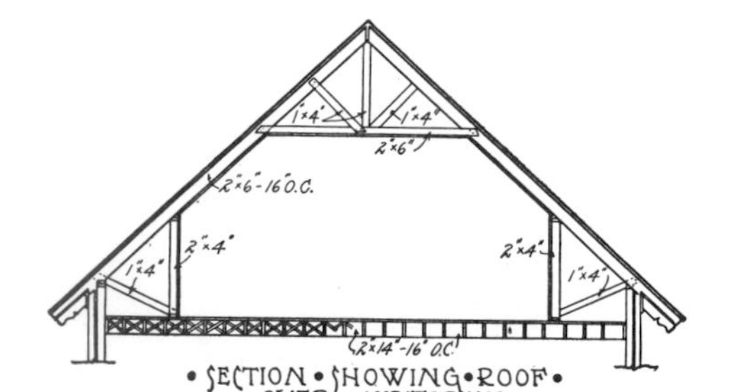

School Building in Wayne, Illinois. The Wide Stairways and Ample Exits Are an Excellent Feature of This Design

A Modern School House for a Small Community

D. E. Postle, Architect, Chicago, Illinois

THE excavation for this building was started in June, 1910, and the entire work was completed in time for the fall term of that year. The base course is of stone, the first story of face brick, and the gables of half timber work. The roofs are covered with shingles. The rooms are light and airy and the feature of having the less-used assembly room on the second floor is a very commendable one. For plans and elevations, see plate following.

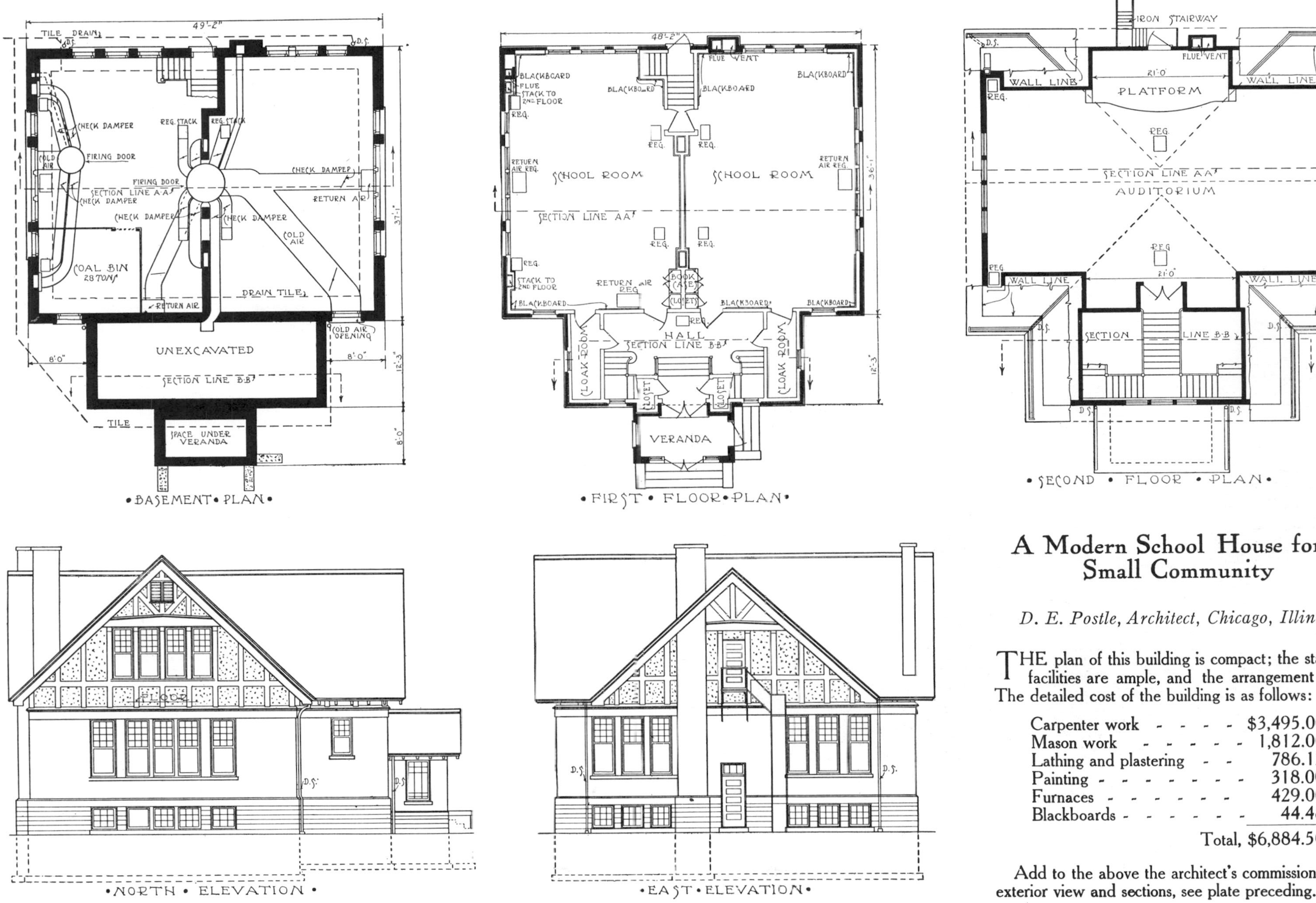

A Modern School House for a Small Community

D. E. Postle, Architect, Chicago, Illinois

THE plan of this building is compact; the stairway facilities are ample, and the arrangement good. The detailed cost of the building is as follows:

Carpenter work - - - -	$3,495.00
Mason work - - - - - -	1,812.00
Lathing and plastering - -	786.12
Painting - - - - - - - -	318.00
Furnaces - - - - - - -	429.00
Blackboards - - - - - - -	44.48
Total,	$6,884.50

Add to the above the architect's commission. For exterior view and sections, see plate preceding.

STACK ROOM
18'-0"×20'-0"
LIBRARIANS ROOM
15'-0"×15'-0"
REFERENCE ROOM
15'-0"×15'-0"
CHILDREN'S READING ROOM
18'-0"×25'-0"
DELIVERY ROOM
16'-0"×25'-0"
GENERAL READING ROOM
18'-0"×25'-0"
TRUSTEES ROOM
15'-0"×15'-0"
LADIES ROOM
15'-0"×15'-0"
DOWN
DOWN
DOWN
DOWN

• FIRST • FLOOR • PLAN •

Public Library at Kearney, New Jersey

Davis, McGrath, and Kiessling, Architects, New York City, New York

AN interesting brick and stone design, the brick laid with Flemish bond. The detail is Greek in character. The Doric order is used with the columns somewhat higher in proportion to their width than is usual, but in this case is very successful. The front faces west. **The building was finished in March, 1907, at a cost of $27,500 complete.**

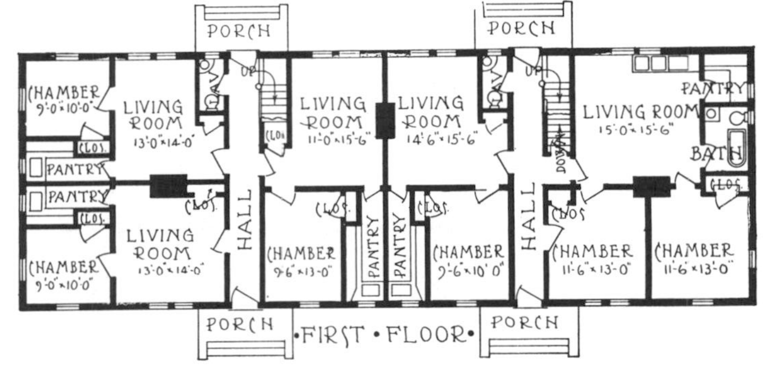

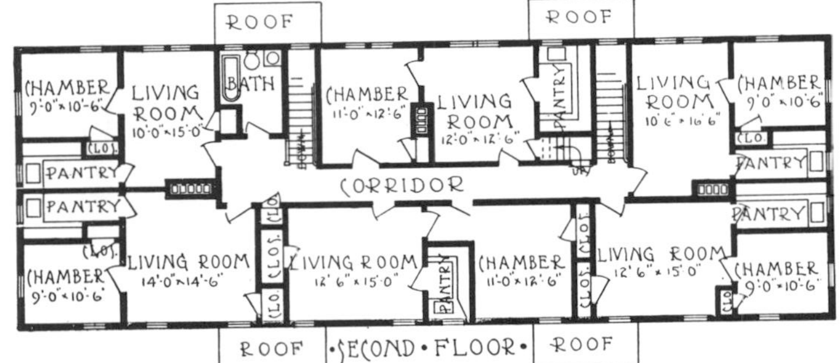

The George Beach Home, Hartford, Connecticut

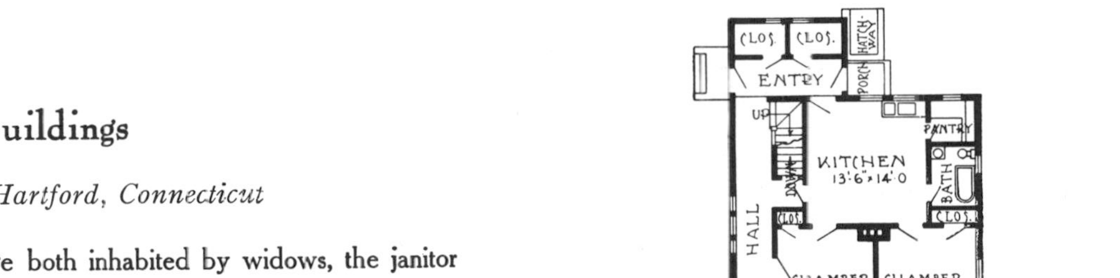

The Long Building Is the George Beach Home, and the Kelsey Memorial Cottage Is Seen on the Right

Institutional Buildings

A. Raymond Ellis, Architect, Hartford, Connecticut

THE Widows' Home and Kelsey Memorial are both inhabited by widows, the janitor occupying the first floor of the Kelsey Memorial. These buildings are finished throughout in gum wood with maple floors. The roofs are of slate. Common brick is used on the lower story of the exterior with black headers, giving a rich texture. The upper story is of stucco. The two homes were built in 1911 and together cost $23,000.

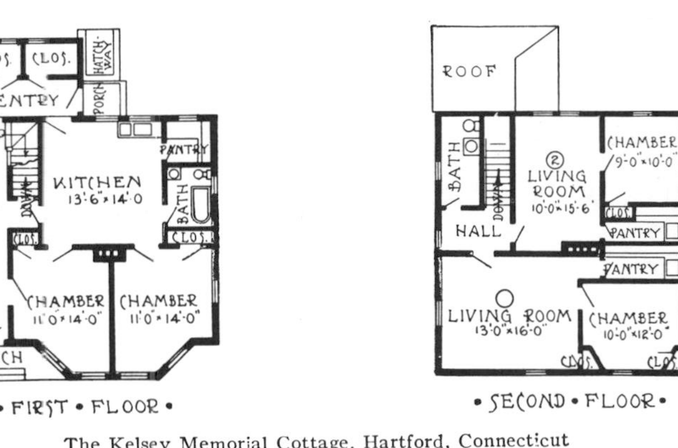

The Kelsey Memorial Cottage, Hartford, Connecticut

Interior Looking Towards Entrance

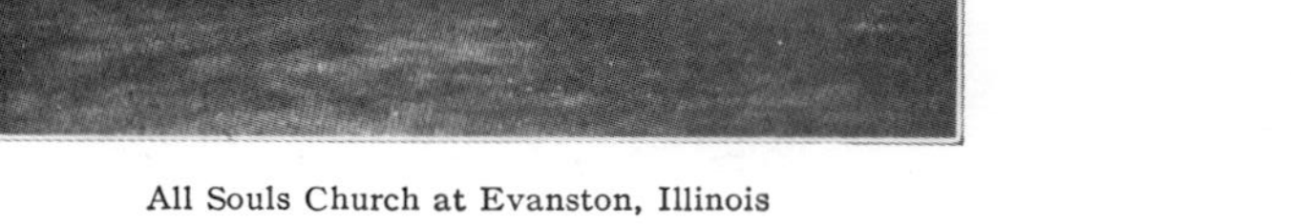

All Souls Church at Evanston, Illinois

Interior Looking Towards Chancel

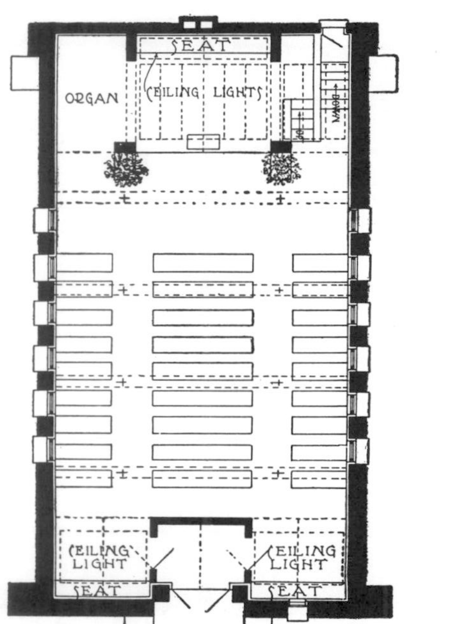

A Small Stone Church of Unusual Merit

Marion M. Griffin, Architect, Chicago, Illinois

THIS attractive little church has a seating capacity of 125. The exterior has been kept as simple and dignified as possible, relying upon the vines to soften the lines of the stone structure. An unusual feature is the art-glass light treatment in the ceiling at the entrance and in the chancel portion. The coloring of the glass is such as to throw a soft light giving an effect of increased height and still preserving a devotional atmosphere about the interior. The leaded glass design in the windows harmonizes with the design in the ceiling lights. The light fixtures and the decorations in the chancel were designed by the architect. The church was built in 1904 at a cost of $6,000, not including the organ. which cost $1,000.

Chancel

Dover Books on Art

GREEK REVIVAL ARCHITECTURE IN AMERICA, T. Hamlin. A comprehensive study of the American Classical Revival, its regional variations, reasons for its success and eventual decline. Profusely illustrated, displaying the work of almost every important architect. 2 appendices. 39 figures, 94 plates containing 221 photos, 62 architectural designs, drawings, etc. 324-item classified bibliography. Index. xi + 439pp. $5\frac{3}{8}$ x $8\frac{1}{2}$.
21148-7 Paperbound $7.50

CREATIVE LITHOGRAPHY AND HOW TO DO IT, Grant Arnold. Written by a man who practiced and taught lithography for many years, this highly useful volume explains all the steps of the lithographic process from tracing the drawings on the stone to printing the lithograph, with helpful hints for solving special problems. Index. 16 reproductions of lithographs. 11 drawings. xv + 214pp. of text. $5\frac{3}{8}$ x $8\frac{1}{2}$.
21208-4 Paperbound $3.50

ARABIC ART IN COLOR, Prisse d'Avennes. 50 full-color plates from rare 19th-century volumes by noted French historian. 141 authentic Islamic designs and motifs from Cairo art treasures include florals, geometrics, Koran illuminations, spots, borders, etc. Ranging from 12th to 18th century, these exquisite illustrations will interest artists, designers of textiles and wallpaper, craftspeople working in stained glass, rugs, etc. Captions. 46pp. $9\frac{3}{8}$ x $12\frac{1}{4}$. 23658-7 Paperbound $6.00

PAINTING IN THE FAR EAST, L. Binyon. A study of over 1500 years of Oriental art by one of the world's outstanding authorities. The author chooses the most important masters in each period—Wu Tao-tzu, Toba Sojo, Kanaoka, Li Lung-mien, Masanobu, Okio, etc.—and examines the works, schools, and influence of each within their cultural context. 42 photographs. Sources of original works and selected bibliography. Notes including list of principal painters by periods. xx + 297pp. $6\frac{1}{8}$ x $9\frac{1}{4}$.
20520-7 Paperbound $5.00

THE ALPHABET AND ELEMENTS OF LETTERING, F. W. Goudy. A beautifully illustrated volume on the aesthetics of letters and type faces and their history and development. Each plate consists of 15 forms of a single letter with the last plate devoted to the ampersand and the numerals. 27 full-page plates. 48 additional figures. xii + 131pp. $7\frac{7}{8}$ x $10\frac{3}{4}$.
20792-7 Paperbound $4.00

THE COMPLETE BOOK OF SILK SCREEN PRINTING PRODUCTION, J. I. Biegeleisen. Here is a clear and complete picture of every aspect of silk screen technique and press operation—from individually operated manual presses to modern automatic ones. Unsurpassed as a guidebook for setting up shop, making shop operation more efficient, finding out about latest methods and equipment; or as a textbook for use in teaching, studying, or learning all aspects of the profession. 124 figures. Index. Bibliography. List of Supply Sources. xi + 253pp. $5\frac{3}{8}$ x $8\frac{1}{2}$.
21100-2 Paperbound $3.50

200 DECORATIVE TITLE-PAGES, edited by A. Nesbitt. Fascinating and informative from a historical point of view, this beautiful collection of decorated titles will be a great inspiration to students of design, commercial artists, advertising designers, etc. A complete survey of the genre from the first known decorated title to work in the first decades of this century. Bibliography and sources of the plates. 222pp. 8⅜ x 11¼.
21264-5 Paperbound $6.00

ON THE LAWS OF JAPANESE PAINTING, H. P. Bowie. This classic work on the philosophy and technique of Japanese art is based on the author's first-hand experiences studying art in Japan. Every aspect of Japanese painting is described: the use of the brush and other materials; laws governing conception and execution; subjects for Japanese paintings, etc. The best possible substitute for a series of lessons from a great Oriental master. Index. xv + 117pp. + 66 plates. 6⅛ x 9¼.
20030-2 Paperbound $5.00

A HANDBOOK OF ANATOMY FOR ART STUDENTS, Arthur Thomson. This long-popular text teaches any student, regardless of level of technical competence, all the subtleties of human anatomy. Clear photographs, numerous line sketches and diagrams of bones, joints, etc. Use it as a text for home study, as a supplement to life class work, or as a lifelong sourcebook and reference volume. Author's prefaces. 67 plates, containing 40 line drawings, 86 photographs—mostly full page. 211 figures. Appendix. Index. xx + 459pp. 5⅜ x 8⅜. 21163-0 Paperbound $7.50

WHITTLING AND WOODCARVING, E. J. Tangerman. With this book, a beginner who is moderately handy can whittle or carve scores of useful objects, toys for children, gifts, or simply pass hours creatively and enjoyably. "Easy as well as instructive reading," N. Y. Herald Tribune Books. 464 illustrations, with appendix and index. x + 293pp. 5½ x 8⅛.
20965-2 Paperbound $4.00

ONE HUNDRED AND ONE PATCHWORK PATTERNS, Ruby Short McKim. Whether you have made a hundred quilts or none at all, you will find this the single most useful book on quilt-making. There are 101 full patterns (all exact size) with full instructions for cutting and sewing. In addition there is some really choice folklore about the origin of the ingenious pattern names: "Monkey Wrench," "Road to California," "Drunkard's Path," "Crossed Canoes," to name a few. Over 500 illustrations. 124 pp. 7⅞ x 10¾. 20773-0 Paperbound $3.25

ART AND GEOMETRY, W. M. Ivins, Jr. Challenges the idea that the foundations of modern thought were laid in ancient Greece. Pitting Greek tactile-muscular intuitions of space against modern visual intuitions, the author, for 30 years curator of prints, Metropolitan Museum of Art, analyzes the differences between ancient and Renaissance painting and sculpture and tells of the first fruitful investigations of perspective. x + 113pp. 5⅜ x 8⅜. 20941-5 Paperbound $2.50

VITRUVIUS: TEN BOOKS ON ARCHITECTURE. The most influential book in the history of architecture. 1st century A.D. Roman classic has influenced such men as Bramante, Palladio, Michelangelo, up to present. Classic principles of design, harmony, etc. Fascinating reading. Definitive English translation by Professor H. Morgan, Harvard. 344pp. $5\frac{3}{8}$ x 8.
20645-9 Paperbound **$4.50**

HAWTHORNE ON PAINTING. Vivid re-creation, from students' notes, of instructions by Charles Hawthorne at Cape Cod School of Art. Essays, epigrammatic comments on color, form, seeing, techniques, etc. "Excellent," Time. 100pp. $5\frac{3}{8}$ x 8.
20653-X Paperbound **$2.25**

THE HANDBOOK OF PLANT AND FLORAL ORNAMENT, R. G. Hatton. 1200 line illustrations, from medieval, Renaissance herbals, of flowering or fruiting plants: garden flowers, wild flowers, medicinal plants, poisons, industrial plants, etc. A unique compilation that probably could not be matched in any library in the world. Formerly "The Craftsman's Plant-Book." Also full text on uses, history as ornament, etc. 548pp. $6\frac{1}{8}$ x $9\frac{1}{4}$.
20649-1 Paperbound **$7.95**

DECORATIVE ALPHABETS AND INITIALS, Alexander Nesbitt. 91 complete alphabets, over 3900 ornamental initials, from Middle Ages, Renaissance printing, baroque, rococo, and modern sources. Individual items copyright free, for use in commercial art, crafts, design, packaging, etc. 123 full-page plates. 3924 initials. 129pp. $7\frac{3}{4}$ x $10\frac{3}{4}$. 20544-4 Paperbound **$5.00**

METHODS AND MATERIALS OF THE GREAT SCHOOLS AND MASTERS, Sir Charles Eastlake. (Formerly titled "Materials for a History of Oil Painting.") Vast, authentic reconstruction of secret techniques of the masters, recreated from ancient manuscripts, contemporary accounts, analysis of paintings, etc. Oils, fresco, tempera, varnishes, encaustics. Both Flemish and Italian schools, also British and French. One of great works for art historians, critics; inexhaustible mine of suggestions, information for practicing artists. Total of 1025pp. $5\frac{3}{8}$ x 8.
20718-8, 20719-6 Two volume set, Paperbound **$15.00**

AMERICAN VICTORIAN ARCHITECTURE, edited by Arnold Lewis and Keith Morgan. Collection of brilliant photographs of 1870's, 1880's, showing finest domestic, public architecture; many buildings now gone. Landmark work, French in origin; first European appreciation of American work. Modern notes, introduction. 120 plates. "Architects and students of architecture will find this book invaluable for its first-hand depiction of the state of the art during a very formative period," ANTIQUE MONTHLY. 152pp. 9 x 12. 23177-1 Paperbound **$6.95**

THE HUMAN FIGURE, J. H. Vanderpoel. Not just a picture book, but a complete course by a famous figure artist. Extensive text, illustrated by 430 pencil and charcoal drawings of both male and female anatomy. 2nd enlarged edition. Foreword. 430 illus. 143pp. $6\frac{1}{8}$ x $9\frac{1}{4}$. 20432-4 Paperbound **$3.00**

Dover Books on Art

THE FOUR BOOKS OF ARCHITECTURE, Andrea Palladio. A compendium of the art of Andrea Palladio, one of the most celebrated architects of the Renaissance, including 250 magnificently-engraved plates showing edifices either of Palladio's design or reconstructed (in these drawings) by him from classical ruins and contemporary accounts. 257 plates. xxiv + 119pp. 9½ x 12¾. 21308-0 Paperbound $10.00

150 MASTERPIECES OF DRAWING, A. Toney. Selected by a gifted artist and teacher, these are some of the finest drawings produced by Western artists from the early 15th to the end of the 18th centuries. Excellent reproductions of drawings by Rembrandt, Bruegel, Raphael, Watteau, and other familiar masters, as well as works by lesser known but brilliant artists. 150 plates. xviii + 150pp. 5⅜ x 11¼. 21032-4 Paperbound $5.00

MORE DRAWINGS BY HEINRICH KLEY. Another collection of the graphic, vivid sketches of Heinrich Kley, one of the most diabolically talented cartoonists of our century. The sketches take in every aspect of human life: nothing is too sacred for him to ridicule, no one too eminent for him to satirize. 158 drawings you will not easily forget. iv + 104pp. 7⅜ x 10¾. 20041-8 Paperbound $3.75

THE TRIUMPH OF MAXIMILIAN I, 137 Woodcuts by Hans Burgkmair and Others. This is one of the world's great art monuments, a series of magnificent woodcuts executed by the most important artists in the German realms as part of an elaborate plan by Maximilian I, ruler of the Holy Roman Empire, to commemorate his own name, dynasty, and achievements. 137 plates. New translation of descriptive text, notes, and bibliography prepared by Stanley Appelbaum. Special section of 10pp. containing a reduced version of the entire Triumph. x + 169pp. 11⅛ x 9¼. 21207-6 Paperbound $5.95

PAINTING IN ISLAM, Sir Thomas W. Arnold. This scholarly study puts Islamic painting in its social and religious context and examines its relation to Islamic civilization in general. 65 full-page plates illustrate the text and give outstanding examples of Islamic art. 4 appendices. Index of mss. referred to. General Index. xxiv + 159pp. 6⅝ x 9¼. 21310-2 Paperbound $6.00

THE MATERIALS AND TECHNIQUES OF MEDIEVAL PAINTING, D. V. Thompson. An invaluable study of carriers and grounds, binding media, pigments, metals used in painting, al fresco and al secco techniques, burnishing, etc. used by the medieval masters. Preface by Bernard Berenson. 239pp. 5⅜ x 8. 20327-1 Paperbound $3.50

THE HISTORY AND TECHNIQUE OF LETTERING, A. Nesbitt. A thorough history of lettering from the ancient Egyptians to the present, and a 65-page course in lettering for artists. Every major development in lettering history is illustrated by a complete aphabet. Fully analyzes such masters as Caslon, Koch, Garamont, Jenson, and many more. 89 alphabets, 165 other specimens. 317pp. 7½ x 10½. 20427-8 Paperbound $5.50